GOD *and the* SOVIETS

by Dr. Marcus Bach

16 pages of photographs by Lorena Bach

If a solution is ever found to the Russian-American deadlock, *God and the Soviets* will help to point the way. Here is a fascinating book, a deeply revealing portrait of the modern Russian mind, interpreted by America's foremost religious researcher.

Before going to Russia, Marcus Bach had visited forty foreign lands, finding in them all that the religious drive is as basic as hunger or love or sex. But Russia remained a riddle, the only country in the world where people are requested openly and without apology to reject belief in God. To try to solve that riddle Dr. Bach and his wife, who took the excellent photographs in the book, went to the U.S.S.R. in 1957.

It is obvious from the book that Dr. Bach is a friendly and approachable man, as well as a skilled reporter. The Russians whom he met, both the people who still devoutly attend church and the atheists, talked to him frankly and openly. He interviewed priests, ministers, and monks and found the exciting story of faith in a country where religion is officially taboo. (It may be surprising to some readers to discover that there are 600,000 members of the Evangelical Baptist Churches of the Soviet Union.)

God and the Soviets

GOD

and the

Soviets

by MARCUS BACH

Thomas Y. Crowell Company
Established 1834   *New York*

Dedicated to those who still believe

that righteousness exalteth a nation.

Third Printing

3 - 87

BS

Contents

Illustrations

The clergy are silent.

"No one hinders us."

One casualty in the rough sea: a broken icon.

FOLLOWING PAGE 118

Women workers shaped the stones with expert skill.

A flower vendor in front of her stall.

The Metro, temple of progress.

The Kremlin.

St. Basil's has kept vigil over the Kremlin for three hundred years.

Prayer was out of fashion.

It was communion service. . . .

Three young students for the Baptist ministry.

"God Be with You till We Meet Again" sung in the Moscow Baptist Church.

Millions have kept their belief.

God and the Soviets

1. The Russian Riddle

I HAD TO GO TO RUSSIA. I could not stay away. My field is religion, religious research, to be exact, and Russia represented a unique, solitary and daring experiment in atheism. This was all I needed to justify my journey.

Only in Russia were people requested openly and without apology to reject belief in God. Only in the U.S.S.R. was spiritual speculation frowned upon and spiritual contemplation disavowed. Only in the land of the Soviets was Christianity and every other living faith with their schedule of rewards for good, punishments for evil, the thrill of the miraculous and the hope of immortality, banned as an impediment in the pursuit of "truth." Only in the vast and sprawling land of the Communists was the abolition of religion a prerequisite for happiness, and the denial of the Divine an evidence of intellectual maturity.

Russia was calling.

Long ago I was told that Marx's famous line, "Religion is the opiate of the people," had been engraved on the walls of Moscow's city hall, opposite the shrine of the Virgin. I never took this idea seriously because I thought it would pass, along with the startling statement of Lenin who said, "God is simply a complex of ideas engendered by the ignorance of mankind."

It did not pass.

A president of the League of Militant Atheists, E. Yaroslavsky, made the Communist position on religion crystal clear, "The conception of the world from the religious point of view is incorrect," he said. "A person cannot act correctly, cannot act in an organized manner as a Communist if his brain is poisoned by religion. Religion is a bandage over the eyes of man, preventing him from seeing the world as it is."

What, I wondered, was happening in Russia now that the bandage had been removed, now that the brain had been rid of the poison? Was Communism actually finding a substitute for all that religion provides in the life of man? Had a new generation arisen with a new code and creed, able to relate such vivid experiences as love, mercy, suffering and joy to a cause and purpose in which God has no recognition and religion plays no part?

I decided to find out for myself. The tangled trails of faith which I had followed in forty foreign lands, the spiritual spoors which had led me into the hallowed precincts of well-known and little-known religions had always led back to the basic tenet that man is by nature spiritual. The religious drive, the urge to worship, the lure of the unknown were as natural as the impulse of hunger or sex or love, as much a part of life as the will to live. I had put them down as universal demonstrations wherever my travels had taken me. I had a favorite saying supported

2

by years of spiritual vagabonding, "Wherever man lives, man worships God." But the whisperings continued that Russia was the incredible exception. Russia was the riddle.

We in America could not grasp the meaning of this experiment in atheism. We could not conceive of it. We would not believe it. I could not believe it because in several Asian nations, Russia's neighbors, men went so far as to say, "Yonder Person, I am He," so close was their identification with God.

In India, philosophers and intellectuals spoke of religion in terms of current events and quoted liberally from their holy books. In the Far East speculation on the mystery of life and death were intimately tied in with everyman's day-by-day experiences. Shintoist, Buddhist, Parsi, Sikh, Jew, Moslem, Christian; whatever path a person followed, it was always a well-worn path and clearly marked. In Africa, in the West Indies, in remote sections of many lands, I found primitive tribes enacting their rituals and performing their rites.

It seemed safe to assume that there were no people in the world who did not foster some kind of "feeling for God" to which they gave expression. I was always saying, "Take away religion and you take away the heart of life." But Russia persisted. Russian atheism persisted. The time had come to find out for myself what was happening to people and religion in the land of the hammer-and-sickle.

So I went to Russia. Lorena, my wife, went with me in the role of photographer as she had done during our research in Haiti, our visit to Albert Schweitzer in Africa, our journeys through the Middle East, our frequent trips to the Doukhobors in Canada and the Maya-Quiches in Guatemala. Her interest was strictly photographic, but she

3

shared with me the feeling that we could never hope to understand Russia or the Russian people until we understood Russian religion or the reason for the lack of it.

Our visas came through in about six weeks. We were advised we had to travel Intourist, the only way one may travel in Russia. Intourist is the Russian government controlled agency that guides and serves every foreign visitor.

I had been told by friends who had traveled in Russia during the days of Stalin (and by others who had never been out of their own town) that Intourist is a plot. It is designed, they insisted, to keep continual watch over travelers, to restrict their actions and spy on their conduct. "You will never get away from your Intourist guides," they warned. "They will search your hotel room. They will let you see just what they want you to see and when they interpret for you, they will tell you just what they want you to hear."

These warnings were subjected to test almost the moment we entered Russian territory.

Our first stop was Leningrad. We arrived in this historic northern city of three million on the midnight train from Helsinki. It had been an easy, comfortable twelve-hour trip of some three hundred miles. We felt no sensation of "dropping behind the Iron Curtain." We encountered no dramatic episodes when we crossed from Finland into the U.S.S.R. The customs and immigration officials who got on at the border station of Vainikkala were business-like and stern, but they did not even bother to examine our luggage. Night fell over us somewhere near Luzhaika. The last daylight scene I remembered was a tiny Russian settlement with a small cemetery and graves marked by blue crosses. "Well," I asked myself, "what did you ex-

4

pect to see? Did you think from all you had heard that even the crosses would be uprooted?" Nearby, in the town, a group of boys were playing and along a country lane workers were going home from the fields carrying rakes and scythes.

It was a Friday night in June when we arrived at the very modern railway station in Leningrad, a station crowded at this late hour with somber, weary travelers, peasant people, working people dressed against the raw cold that greeted us. The men wore black woolen suits and tight-fitting caps; the women were bundled up in heavy, nondescript coats with dark scarves tied tightly over their heads. Almost everyone carried a pack of some kind or sat or slept near a bundle of belongings.

We were met by a young, scholarly Russian from Intourist. He was an attractive, blond Moscovite and might have been a student from any western college. An excellent linguist, he spoke fluent English and made us feel at home by the frequent use of an American idiom, "Okay." "What say we go?"

We went by taxi to the Astoria Hotel through wide, straight streets devoid of cars, but rather well filled with people, workers for the most part going or coming from their jobs.

Vladimir, our guide, had no apparent curiosity about us, but a great interest in doing his job and making our welcome as pleasant as possible at this past-midnight hour. As we rode along he advised us about the time for breakfast, hoped we would find the Astoria Hotel comfortable and urged me to suggest any wishes I might have for getting the utmost out of our three-day stay in Leningrad.

I explained to him that my interest was religion. To this

5

he said, "Very well, let me know if I can help you in any way." So I asked him for the names of churches, advice on meeting church leaders and other information in this field. All of which he said he would do his best to supply. Did he go to church? No, never.

As we approached the large, modern six-story Astoria Hotel, I noticed a magnificent cathedral nearby whose immense gilded dome glistened in the night and whose wide granite steps and huge columns reminded me of the Capitol building in Washington. Scaffolding was rigged up within the porticoes. The colossal doors were barred with workmen's ladders.

"What church is that?" I asked.

"St. Isaac's Cathedral," he answered promptly. "It is being repaired. It is a museum."

"A museum? Don't people worship there any more?"

"It is a museum," he repeated and I decided it was too late at night to begin any serious research.

However, next morning, immediately after a sumptuous eight o'clock breakfast which included caviar and fried eggs, yogurt and excellent sweet rolls, I was eager to get started. Vladimir appeared on time. When I told him I wanted to take a walk alone and get a feeling for the city, his reply was, "Very well, don't get lost." Lorena was also free and on her own to go scouting for pictures, so I felt that the warnings of my friends about Intourist had been grossly exaggerated or deliberately distorted.

I certainly felt unrestricted and free, and I sallied forth with the "guide" I have always secretly depended upon in my research: a good destiny.

It was not only Saturday morning in Leningrad; it was the 250th anniversary of the founding of the city.

Flags and banners and story-high pictures of Russian officials, members of the Presidium, decorated the town. Red flags, bright with the gold star and emblazoned with the hammer and sickle, were everywhere. Loudspeakers blared out music and shrieked forth announcements of coming events, promising parades and military displays.

All of Russia seemed to be streaming into Leningrad and all of Russia looked like members of the working class. They were on holiday, strolling along the banks of the Neva River, gathering in the parks, lining the canal bridges which give this old city something of the flavor of Venice. They never so much as paused to observe the outsider who had come to find out how they worship or what they believe.

To them I was another visitor, and to me they were like people anywhere in the world, in a city sacred to their hearts. For this metropolis of aristocratic homes and magnificent public buildings was once St. Petersburg, founded by Peter the Great in 1707. He built the Admiralty with its moat and gilded spire. He planned the Winter Palace, the Summer Palace, monasteries and cathedrals. These belonged to the tsar and to succeeding tsars and tsarinas. This was the tsars' city until the 1917 Revolution when, in one well-planned and flaming conquest, it became the property of *the people* and was renamed Leningrad in honor of the people's liberator, Vladimir Ilyanov Lenin.

Were the people better off now? Why, yes. They walked where Peter walked. They were allowed to roam the marble halls of the palace he had built for Catherine and the parks and palaces in which he entertained the visiting kings. They could see the robes he wore and touch the books he read and stand before the painted masterpieces he had

7

hoarded. When Peter built the city he said, "I want a window to look out upon the world!" And now the *people* stood at this "window" and the *people* walked through the bastille and the *people* paraded on the famous street called *October Prospekt* remembering that on October 25 in 1917 the Bolsheviki set them free.

I had walked about a mile from the hotel when I stopped to ask directions from two young Russians. My Russian vocabulary was as bad as their English, so we settled for German. They were brother and sister, students, they informed me, in the field of engineering and were on the way home from their examinations.

The fact that I was an American was all they needed to bombard me with questions. What was I doing in Russia? Did I like Leningrad? Did America really want war? How tall is our tallest skyscraper? What kind of home did I live in?

When I told them my interest was religion, the young man exclaimed, "We have churches here." He said this as if to correct immediately the charge that Communism had closed the places of worship.

"Do you go to church?" I asked.

His answer showed surprise. "I? No. Never."

I put the same question to his sister.

"I have never been inside a church," she said, and her voice and manner indicated I should have known the answer in advance. She dismissed the subject by asking, "Is it true that American students are taught to hate Russia?"

We moved back against a building where we could talk without being an annoyance to the crowds who walked the streets. I informed them that, as far as I knew, no one in

America was being taught or requested to hate anyone. She wanted to believe me, but she was not sure. She had heard about American "hate campaigns." I had not. She had been told we wanted to fight Russia. I had not.

We got back to the subject of religion.

"What is a religious museum?" I asked. "I mean a church like St. Isaac's Cathedral?"

"Oh, that," said the young man almost eagerly, "is the preservation of a church by the government so that we can learn how people used to think about religion and what they used to do with religion."

"The government closes a church for worship and opens it as a museum?" I asked.

"The state preserves it," he replied. "There are enough churches that are open."

"For worship?"

"Of course, for worship."

"How is it you have never been inside a church?"

His dark eyes flashed. "Churches," he proclaimed, "are for old people. Many old people believe in religion and need it. We do not believe in it. We do not need it."

"Why don't you need it?"

"Why do I?" he countered in a serious, puzzled voice. Then in a sudden, dramatic outburst, he declared, "I have beliefs to live up to! I have a religion!" Impressively he added, "This!" and with an impassionate gesture indicated the moving crowds.

He stood there, a dominating figure, lost for a moment in the enthusiasm of his role. He held his pose while his sister watched him half-amused, half-enthralled. He clasped his books impetuously in his hands while the crowds went by—the poorly dressed citizens of Leningrad, the peasants who had come in for the anniversary celebration, the shoppers who lined up in queues in the doorways of the stores and came out clutching their meager purchases—his people, his greatest belief. Did I understand? His first and major belief was in the people, in Mother Russia. This was his religion. These were his code and creed.

All this time the loudspeakers urged the masses to remember that once Leningrad had been in ruins. Once for two and a half years it had been walled about by Hitler's guns and had refused to die. They were being reminded that thousands had given their lives to save this city; that other thousands had died of hunger; that ten years ago death and terror walked these streets while today, if they but listened, they could hear music and singing, and if they but looked, they could see a new and greater Leningrad rising and a new and greater Russia being born.

I say this was my first "religious" encounter in Russia because this young man was obviously a zealot. He might as well have been a Fulton Sheen or a Billy Graham, he was just as convinced about his vocation and equally dogmatic about his views. There was no doubt about it, he had found his faith and was ready to tell the world. Could it be, I wondered, that young Communists actually feel they have to forget God in order to remember the people? Was this student a symbol of his generation? Would most of Russia's 230 million people reflect his fervor and echo his creed: Communism is my religion and the state is my God!

My research had a creed, too. It had always maintained that "God necessarily exists" and the theory had followed from definition and awareness. But here in the U.S.S.R. I was now finding fresh, eager, earnest, cultured young people who defied both my awareness and my definition.

In Russia's race against the world, had it really stripped itself of religion in order to be better fitted for the running?

"Come with us to our home," the girl was saying. "Come and tell us about America. Leave religion to the religionists. Let us talk about things we can do something about. Why does not your country stop making the H-bomb? We are all for peace. Look, there is a sign for peace and there is another."

She was right about that. *Mir* (Peace) was blazoned on streamers above doorways and printed on window cards and written on the pictures of Russian leaders. *Mir* was even spelled out with cookies in a bakery window.

"You see," said the young man as we made our way through the crowds, "we cannot stop making bombs until America stops. That is only being realistic." He glanced at me and smiled wisely as if to say, "Your country is realistic, too, is it not?" Or perhaps he was asking, "Where does religion enter into this? Who should trust the other first, do you suppose? Should the Christian first trust the Communist, or the Communist first trust the Christian?"

Now we were approaching a cathedral built in the form of a huge cross. It looked like an ambitious attempt to copy St. Peter's in Rome, complete with a tremendous semicircle of towering colonnades forming a miniature Vatican Square.

"Kazan Cathedral," said my companions. Then the young man added surreptitiously, "It's a museum, you know."

I did not know. I asked, "Is it open?"

"Of course."

"St. Isaac Museum is closed for repairs. I tried to get in early this morning."

11

"Kazan is open. Open and free."

"You have been there?"

"Oh, yes," they replied together.

"It will be on my list," I said confidently.

I meant the list I had requested from Intourist, but when I thought about it I wondered whether such information or help would actually be forthcoming. There was no reason to doubt it, but I did. For, suddenly, as we walked, I had the impression that Russia did not ring true. There was no reason for this feeling, none that I could define. It was simply intuitive. Or maybe it was the sight of the cathedral turned into a museum. Or perhaps the echoing voices of friends back home who had sent me off with warnings and words of caution, "Don't trust the Russians. Don't believe the Russians. The Godless can never be good."

Whatever it was, I saw the slowly moving traffic— meager automobile traffic with a few droshkies (horse-drawn carriages) thrown in—and the traffic cops, several of whom were women, and the long queues in front of the stores, and the group of soldiers marching, no doubt to join the anniversary parade. I absorbed it all and had the feeling that everyone was a captive and no one was expressing his true individuality. Even my engineering students, Anton and Olga, despite Anton's dramatic stand in the city street, seemed to be playing a role behind which their real selves were secretly and skilfully concealed. Suddenly I wondered if *I* were really free and if my trip could actually be as easy and as unrestricted as it seemed. Was I being watched and followed? Was there someone in the crowd who had his eye on me? Prodded by these thoughts I glanced back quickly over my shoulder.

A dark-haired, hatless young man with open shirt

caught my eye. He was directly behind me, practically on my heels.

"American?" he asked eagerly with an accent.

We stopped.

"Anything to sell?" he pleaded. "Clothes? Suit? Stockings? Where you stay? What is number of your room?"

Olga got quickly into the scene. "Go along," she said to him in Russian. "Aren't you ashamed of yourself?"

He looked at her for a moment, hurt and confused, then walked away into the crowds.

"A foolish boy," she said with an exaggerated sigh, as though we should all forgive him. "He thought you might have American clothes which you did not need and which he could buy cheaper than the things sold in our stores."

With this she linked an arm in mine and an arm in her brother's and led us into a side street away from the crowds. She laughed and talked, thrilled to think that an American was to visit their home, while all the while I repented a bit because of my apparently ill-founded suspicions.

Their home was a two-room apartment with adjoining bath, up five outside flights in a building whose gray brick walls still showed the gouged-out wounds of World War II. The place was dark and scantily furnished. The small room which we entered from a gloomy hallway served as kitchen and dining room. A larger room with windows looking down on the court provided a place for study and sleeping quarters with three cots. I was told that the mother of the students also lived here, that she was employed in a garment factory, and that sister and brother also worked— in stores—during their off school hours.

This type of family, I learned from Olga and Anton,

is representative of many in which the father died during the defense of Russia at the time of the Nazi invasion. In fact, I soon realized we cannot quite understand Russia without taking family units of this kind into account. Russia lost 7,500,000 men in World War II and when we see women doing men's work on Russian streets and in factories, it is because an entire generation of men has been annihilated. Their sons and daughters have picked up life out of the rubble and salvaged hope out of the devastation, and if they are living in horror of another war it is because they are still haunted by the last. They have the right to be afraid. They also have a right and a need to be self-sufficient and serious about the future. Education with them is a passion.

They feel they must be experts in every field and surpass every other nation in order to survive. Inconveniences and absence of luxuries are discounted with a wave of the hand as inconsequential and unrelated to their goal, a goal which they describe as "the Russia we are building." They give you the impression they are willing to suffer and sacrifice and serve in the building of it, and they want you to believe and know that with them this constitutes a living faith. These are the people, not the leaders. These are the masses, not the masters. These are the Russians, not Russia.

But what about religious faith as we think of it, faith in God, a personal relationship with God, the ideal of brotherhood based on the divinity in men, all men? What about the principles and ideals and loyalties and demands commonly associated with religious faith?

The search for an answer to these questions made my visit with these students important. They represented not only a type of family, but a type of mind. They lived like

14

millions of other young Russians are living, and they thought the way millions of Russian young people are thinking.

They are afraid of religion. They do not trust religion. They have been taught to suspect institutionalized religion of intrigue and exploitation. They consider religion rank sentimentality, primitive superstition, a form of class oppression, a symptom of bourgeois reactionism. They believe that the conduct of so-called religious people belies the concepts professed. Christians, they insist, are worse than non-Christians because of a tendency to justify their actions on the basis of "divine authority." Christians, they believe, are usually hypocrites. Here, in these students, I had my first frank introduction to a generation of young intellectuals who have consistently been taught the weaknesses and wickedness of religion more thoroughly than our American young people have ever been taught its merits and its worth.

As I sat in this Russian home answering questions about my country, discussing religion and getting a close look into the hearts of two of Mother Russia's children, I realized that their misinformation about us and our way of life was appalling. Not only did they know nothing about the constructive work of the church, the social and spiritual outreach of religion, the meaning of the Christian ethic, or the church's place in our cultural scheme, they knew startlingly little about American life in the areas where we feel Russia is particularly interested.

For example, they knew nothing about our labor-management relationships, feeling compelled to ask whether the worker ever got anywhere without a strike. Their basic information about American home life was that one out of every five couples is divorced. Their knowledge of American youth was limited to statistics on juvenile delinquency and our sky-rocketing crime rate, figures which, by the way, were all too accurate. Racism was a big issue with them, for they had heard of lynchings and race riots and of Negroes dying of hunger on the streets of New York City and riots related to integration in Southern schools. They had heard the worst about the worst in us and not a word about the good in us. But they were up on American classical literature and versed in American history and familiar with American politics.

No research is ever devoid of some deep-seated preconceived ideas. I can never fully rid myself of them, and I admit I held some points of view about Russian young people which needed early reappraisal. I confess I had a suspicion that since Russian young people do not believe in God, neither do they believe in goodness. It had been drummed into me long and hard in my parental Protestant church and spelled out in graphic examples by preachers and priests that those who have no religion may be suspected of having no morals. But Anton and Olga obviously had morals. They had culture and refinement by any standard, and I was certainly being contemptible if I presumed to judge them. They had love for each other, love for their mother and, as I had already seen, love for their nation. They had love for learning and love for life. I had a feeling they even had a certain concern for my America.

They sought to convince me that Communism was unmistakably their ideal and that the vocation of their lives was interwoven with the state. They claimed to respect and admire the present party bosses and felt these bosses were rather perfectly carrying out the will of the people.

For the capitalistic system and private enterprise they had only a sorrowful shake of the head and incredible wonder that a people as enlightened as Americans could not see how outmoded and shot through with evil our "Christian materialism" actually is. Compared with Marxist materialism, it is unjust, unreliable and grossly unrelated to the modern era. So they said.

What, I asked, did they think about America's interest in the welfare of other nations, the churches' concern for other people, the Americans' philanthropies to other individuals? "These things are not philanthropic," they replied. "They are opportunistic." What about our standard of living and the opportunities Americans enjoy? Are these related in any way to what we believe? "No. You are a young country and you have prospered while other countries have suffered and been destroyed." What about the fact that our system out-produces, out-invents, out-supplies the Communistic system? The answer was, "Give us time."

Often as they looked at me I sensed a secret longing, a hope, a wish that they might see for themselves just what our country is like, just how we live, just why we believe as we do. They had come a long way, these young Russians, a long way since the days of the tsars a short half-century ago. They are part of the thought and life of their people now. They have books which once only the most privileged enjoyed, and opportunities to learn which once were restricted to the aristocracy, and they can sit and talk freely and express their own ideas and, who can say how much they dare to dream?

"Anton," I asked, "don't you have a secret curiosity or hunger for what religion does in the individual life?"

He was not to be taken off guard. "I know what it does," he exclaimed. "That is why I do not trust it."

Olga and I laughed at this reasoning, for he stubbornly refused to admit he might have lost his objectivity.

I then asked him what he thought of Jesus.

"A myth," he said flatly. "Truly a myth. And be glad He is. If He were real it would be even worse to think of the wars fought in His name and the cruelty and oppression He has caused, to say nothing of the divisions He is responsible for among the people."

Olga agreed. "The wars we had to fight were against religious people. Christian rulers and the church were always the oppressors."

I suggested we would have to call in the historians and theologians to settle this, but Anton said flatly, "What is past is past and what may have been is only speculation."

"Heaven and hell and God are all speculation," Olga added.

"And belief in *no* God is not speculation?" I asked.

"Let us deal with concrete matters," Anton argued. "How can America and Russia understand each other?"

"Perhaps by meeting each other," I answered. "By sitting down together as we are doing."

"America does not want to sit down with us," he retorted. "Some people believe that guided missiles will do away with war because they will make war so terrible. That I do not believe. War has always been terrible but still there are wars. Peace can come only through mutual trust."

"And mutual trust is a product of faith," I said.

"That is right. But not faith according to the old state religions. Faith between men."

"And faith in God?" I asked.

"I do not know what you mean," he said with an exaggerated sigh. "I have never seen a god nor heard a god—"

"—nor had a feeling for God?" I prodded. "Don't you ever have the sense of nearness to something higher and greater than yourself?"

"Of course," he answered enthusiastically. "But why should I think of that as God? It is simply my thought of the good and the beautiful. Maybe it is my thought of a better life for all people. Let us not be superstitious. If I start creating gods, someone else starts creating gods, and soon one god is fighting another god. That is the history of religion. It is the struggle of one man's god against another man's god."

Here he rested his case, and Olga served us tea and cakes, and I was asked if I had any questions or comments. And I said, "Well, you see, Anton, if Communism rules out God because He is hypothetical, I have the same right to rule him in. If you reject Him because of the injustices done in His name, I accept Him because of the blessings He has brought. And if Russia denies Him because He has been responsible for a tradition of enslavement, America, by the same token, accepts Him because He has given us our tradition of freedom."

There I rested my case and Anton said thoughtfully, "Well, well." And we enjoyed the cakes and tea.

Then they presented me with a gift, a small gold pin commemorating Leningrad's anniversary on which was engraved, *"Mir Miru"* (peace in all the world). The best

19

I had to offer them in return for this kindness were some bright and shining Lincoln pennies which I had brought to Russia as tokens of friendship. They knew the story and the details of Lincoln's life and were thrilled at the unexpected gift. They examined one of the coins closely and Anton exclaimed with enthusiasm, "Look! 'In God We Trust!' "

"More propaganda," I said, and they laughed at this and wanted to know whether "propaganda" of this sort appeared on all American coins. I said I thought it did, though we omitted it from our paper currency. Anton murmured, "A-ha! Now that is something to figure out!"

We said our good-bys, but they then decided to help me locate a taxi, for the hotel was some distance away.

I did not go to the hotel. I went to Kazan Cathedral, because the "Museum of Religion" and the sight of the replica of St. Peter's had stayed in my mind. Intourist might put the place on my list, but something was luring me to visit it at once.

Hundreds of Russians evidently had the same urge. A queue had formed in front of the huge bronze doors when my taxi brought me there. I was soon to learn that four thousand visitors go through these doors each day to see "what religion is and does" or, better, "what religion was and did" in the lives of the people.

Anton had said, "Kazan is open and free," but he had not prepared me for the macaber splendor of the cathedral interior. A kaleidoscopic flash of impressions hit me all at once as I stepped inside. First of all, there was the sense of garish disorder, almost distortion, of a disarray of religious paintings, frescoes, statues, icons, and reliquaries of all kinds.

Then there was the overwhelming sight of row upon row of Corinthian columns, all seeming to converge upon a series of piers which, in turn, supported the huge dome with a kind of dizzy motion, while a tremendously high balustrade encircled most of the nave, and a sanctuary with monolithic pillars stood like the entrance to a holy of holies—only this holy of holies had been defamed with statues and paintings depicting religion as a merciless taskmaster and tyrant. For example, there was the huge picture of peasants bearing a golden cross on top of which sat a pudgy capitalist smoking a cigar and whipping the people as they followed the figure of Christ.

There were guides to serve me, but I preferred to walk alone in the first cathedral dedicated to atheism that I had ever been in. I learned from placards that it took ten years to build this church and that it was completed in 1811. It served the Russian Orthodox faith for some 125 years before the Communists put their interdict upon it and "preserved" it as a museum. The people built it, the tsars ruled it, the priests served it, the Communists own it—in the name of the people.

Here on this site Catherine II was crowned. Here emperors came to pray. Here Cossacks worshiped and peasants bowed before the icon of the Wonder-Working Virgin of Kazan. Here Alexander I spent his night of prayer before his battle with Napoleon and here he knelt after he returned victoriously from his campaign.

These are but phantom memories, blotted out by pictures of debauched priests and nuns and the paintings of Christ the oppressor, Christ directing the Horses of the Apocalypse as they grind the people under their hooves. I was on a journey into the evolution of faith, but it was only one part of faith's story, the part that deals with religion's atrocities, extravagances, and follies. It depicted not what religion did to uplift mankind, but what man had done to degrade religion in his darkest moments. This was what it was. A snake pit of the defamation of religion. A warped, one-sided, insidiously distorted portraiture of faith.

I went down into a lower level to see the part played by the Inquisition, to gaze at religion's torture chambers and religion's instruments of terror. Everything was authentic, from the branding irons to the stretching-rack. I gazed silently at life-sized wax figures of "martyrs," made more horrible and stark by theatrical lighting.

I walked around viewing scenes from other bloody chapters in the frightful fable of faith: horror scenes from the Thirty Years' War, obscenities from the period of the Reformation, torture practices of the Counter Reformation. A portrait of a Pope showed the head of a mule. Caricatures of priests, paintings of pretenders, princes and patriarchs set forth the story of how these individuals defiled men through their domination of the church. I stood face to face with historical evidence that peasants were whipped and then baptized, while others were baptized and then killed in the name of Christ.

I paused transfixed before instruments of maceration: iron shackles, iron chains, hair shirts, iron crosses with ball and chain which penitents once willingly embraced in order to appease a jealous and demanding God. I saw the picture of Christ with the caption, "A Jewish Fortune-teller." I found the story of the crucifixion retold in paintings and sculptured pieces so devised as to impress upon the viewer the dictates of a God who demanded the blood and the

Church domes rose upward. . . .

Representation of a young Russian mother, clasping a child in her arms and struggling, ready to fall, under the killing weight of an overpowering iron cross.

There was a statue that fascinated me: the huge bronze figure of a man with a cross looming like a colossus high above the Dnieper.

The work of a hundred years and the labor of ten thousand hands were turned to desolation between the hours of dusk and dawn.

The two were charmers and they knew it.

Communism is starkly real, fiercely contemporary, having in it ideas that all too often answer to youth's deepest disillusionment and gravest discontent.

Schools, but not Sunday schools, have caught the imagination of young Marxists.

People are free to avail themselves of church ceremonies, but informed atheism has grown so powerful psychologically that many worshipers are shamed into staying away from church.

The clergy of the Russian Orthodox Church are not prepared to say one word against the government.

"Are you free to propagate the faith?" I asked. "Why shouldn't we be? No one hinders us."

My casualty in the rough sea was one broken icon.

death of His only Son. Placards asked me to consider whether in the history of Russia there was ever a personage more cruel than Yahweh or even a political intrigue more monstrous than this "myth" with which the masses were once oppressed. "Freedom, freedom!" was the call of Kazan. "Freedom from religion! Freedom from the farce of faith! Linger here and let God go!"

Kazan, where priests once chanted and worshipers bowed in prayer; Kazan, the Cathedral of the Virgin, is now a house of terror for those who knew it when it was the House of God. This is what has happened to St. Isaac's and to countless other great cathedrals throughout the U.S.S.R. "But don't you see," the visitors seem to say as they wend their way through the ever-crowded aisles, "it is all true. This is religion's unexpurgated story. Here you see how it rose crudely in the dull mind of the primitive with his sacrifices and followed an unbroken line to the sacrifice of Christ. Here are the statues and the histories of animistic religions, folk religions, Greek, Roman, Christian religions—now at last you see how they are links in the agonizing chain that has poisoned men's minds since the beginning of time."

In the sanctuary, near the sacred doors, where one of the most beautiful iconostases in all Russia was revered, where the monolithic columns rise, Communism has placed a huge, artistically sculptured piece. It is the representation of a young Russian mother. She is clasping a child in her arms and is struggling, ready to fall, under the killing weight of a huge iron cross. The story is complete. There is no ambiguity here. The history of religion has been told and it is being retold each day to those who step inside the Cathedral of Kazan.

I had a strange, lingering feeling when I emerged once more into the light of day. In my sentimental way, I felt that God had only loaned Kazan to the Soviets and that He was actually standing in the shadows, preserving the cathedral for some great and final denouement. I had to remind myself that those shadows are deep, but for a hypnotic moment, remembering that His power is active and vital in the life of man, since He does move and act in history and has survived history itself, I wondered if He might not return once more as a psychological and social force to Russian life? Can belief in Him ever be sublimated into belief in the state? Is it possible for man to build a moral order strictly upon the concept of a "people's republic?" Has Russia found a substitute and an answer for man's age-long spiritual quest?

I pursued the riddle further after reporting in at the hotel and urging Lorena to go to Kazan Cathedral for pictures. She had put in some exciting hours at the Hermitage, the once fabulous palace of Catherine II which today is the Louvre of Russia and the show place of Leningrad. It is filled with rare art treasures, including originals by da Vinci, Botticelli, Angelico, Andrea del Sarto, Titian, Filippino Lippi and every other artist of every other classical school. It features Giordano's "Descent from the Cross," Ribera's "Christ with the Crown of Thorns" and El Greco's "Apostles Peter and Paul."

Lorena had run into her own bit of religious adventuring in the Hermitage. In a room in which the wall space was covered with fifteenth-century Italian paintings, she found herself standing beside an unusually well-dressed, middle-aged Russian gentleman who tried out his English and became her traveling companion through several other exhibit rooms. He was as eager to talk to an American as Lorena was to learn more about him. For he said he came often to the Hermitage on his day off from work as a consulting engineer.

When they arrived at the third floor and Lorena was overwhelmed by the vast collection of the French impressionists, she remarked to her Russian friend, "Here are originals by Gauguin and Van Gogh and Matisse which I never even knew existed!"

The Russian smiled tolerantly, unable to understand her enthusiasm.

"Do you really like these?" he inquired. "I see that you do. But we do not. Look around. You will see no Russians in these rooms."

Lorena suggested that the Russian taste had perhaps not been cultivated and that modern painting had not evolved under Russian Communism. He was interested in her observation and after some discussion about art, Lorena mentioned our reason for coming to Russia. He said to her, "Why doesn't your husband come to church with me tomorrow?"

"Do you belong to a church?" Lorena asked, surprised.

He smiled and said, "Yes, I do. You see, I was born before the Revolution."

So she made a Sunday morning date for me and when I mentioned this to my Intourist guide he said in a very matter-of-fact way, "So, you have a chance to go to church. Which church?"

"A Russian Orthodox," I said. "St. Nikolai."

And he said, "Okay."

I thought again that Intourist was everything I could ask for in the way of cooperation, an opinion which was more than justified when he said, "Oh, by the way, the Service Bureau will give you the list you requested."

The hotel's Service Bureau, which is also a government agency, was as courteous as Intourist. Its business is to aid travelers, and just now the four girls who operated it were busy with delegations from China, Burma, Pakistan, and Czechoslovakia who were on hand for Leningrad's anniversary celebration. Just ahead of me in the queue was a group of young Germans from East Berlin. They were on a two-weeks sightseeing tour. Equipped with cameras and flashguns, dressed like western tourists, they convinced me they were not nearly as captive as I had been led to believe. In fact, one of the party said to me in an exaggerated whisper, "Where is this Iron Curtain? Who put it up? We travel everywhere freely with the exception of America."

I reached the Service Bureau desk and the girl handed me a list of churches. In excellent English she assured me the Bureau would be happy to help me further in any way. Incidentally, while I had the chance, I inquired about tickets for an opera or ballet or symphony. Everything was sold out, even the "world-famous" puppet show which had come to Leningrad from Moscow. I told her I was especially sorry about that. I'd give anything to see the puppet show!

"Just a moment," she said. "Let me see what I can do." After considerable telephoning, she advised me she had got hold of two tickets. I tried to overpay her, but she refused and seemed a bit offended, bearing out what I had often heard about the Russian attitude toward tipping.

The list she handed me included the names of one Roman Catholic church, one Moslem mosque, five Russian Orthodox churches and the Kazan Museum of Religion. I asked about Protestant churches and was told that the Bureau would try to get the information for me. I requested the names of religious leaders and was told that perhaps I would have a better chance to meet church officials when I arrived in Moscow. So I decided to devote Sunday to churchgoing, beginning with six o'clock early Mass at the Roman Catholic service, following this with a visit to the Russian Orthodox church if Lorena's "friend from the Hermitage" kept his promise to pick me up.

Early Sunday morning I took a cab to the Roman Catholic church. The building was poor and in need of repair. The church, small, cold and dark, was occupied by no more than fifty worshipers, elderly peasant women and one old man who incessantly rocked back and forth in his pew mumbling, *"Dominus vobiscum."*

An air of hopelessness hung over this early-morning service. It seemed a futile, dying attempt to perpetuate the faith. The elevated wooden pulpit looked as if it had been abandoned long ago. The stations of the cross were dusty. The priest and his assistant, elderly and devout, performed the age-old ritual as if it were the one remaining tenuous link between God and the people. When the white embroidered altar cloth was placed over the railing and the faithful advanced, when the chanting of the small choir stirred our hearts, I had the feeling that I was worshiping somewhere at the ends of the earth. But I also felt that to each humble participant faith was desperately precious and the hope for a miracle of religious rebirth had not yet died. The acolyte held the lighted candle. The lowly priest took the bread and laid it upon the tongue of the penitent. Behind me the old man continued to murmur his doleful, *"Dominus vobiscum."* The communicants returned to their

27

pews with folded hands and transfigured faces as if the light of hope had been rekindled in their hearts.

But the most interesting feature about my first service in the U.S.S.R. was a memorable, though hurried, talk with the priest who told me in effect that, "The work of the Church is full of promise in Russia!" And in answer to the question, "Are you enjoying religious freedom?" he replied, "Why, of course. We are most surely free. There is complete separation of church and state. The future of the Church is up to us."

This impressive, though ambiguous, statement was one I resolved to check against the opinion of other religious leaders during my Russian stay. Is the pursuit of religion "surely free"? Is the separation between church and state complete? And is it possible that the future of the Church is actually in the hands and hearts of the people who believe?

Lorena's friend was waiting at the hotel when I returned. He was waiting in his Pobeda automobile, a small Russian-built car, and he was obviously pleased that he could be of service to an American. In fact his fondest wish was to visit the United States. That, he feared, would be impossible. He was not a Communist but he felt certain that his government would give him a visa. He felt he could even afford to come; however, he had the feeling that America would not want him to come. Why? He could not say. He simply felt he was not welcome. He had the haunting apprehension that he would be mistreated. He hoped relations between Russia and America would improve and then, perhaps, his feelings, too, would change.

As we drove together to the Cathedral of St. Nikolai, he talked freely about his position as technical adviser in an electrical plant, a job that paid him 1800 rubles a month, the equivalent of about a hundred and eighty American dollars. He was not complaining about that. It was standard governmental wage in a country where everything was governmental. His car was paid for. Of course, it was. Did anyone in Russia buy anything "on time"? *Nyet.* Few people had cars, so he was fortunate in this respect. His Pobeda had cost him 20,000 rubles. He had to work more than a year for that. A suit cost him 1000 to 1800 rubles. A necktie, 60 rubles. Shoes, 300 rubles. Rent was reasonable, about five per cent of his salary. He was living well according to Russian standards, but there were, of course, other standards in the world. He was not complaining, understand. But it was too bad he had such a feeling about going to America. It would be interesting to see how people live in the United States and to discover how much a technician with his training could earn. He had heard some engineers received as much as $10,000 a year. Even more?

I asked him the question, "Is there complete separation of church and state?" He said, "Yes, I suppose one would say there is." I inquired whether he believed that Russian people are free to worship. He replied, "Yes, I would say so, but, of course, Communist Party members are not allowed to belong to a church." I asked whether he felt that the future of religion is "up to the people" or whether there might be governmental pressure to limit worship and the churches' growth. To this he said, "The future of religion is always up to the people."

When we drew up to the curb in front of the imposing Russian Orthodox church whose domes and gleaming pillars spoke of dignity and charm, I realized at once that my friend was no doubt an exceptional member. For one thing, his car was the only one on the street. And no sooner had we gone inside the spacious churchyard, through the iron gateway, than it was obvious he was one of the few worshipers not of peasant stock. Some seventy or more black-scarved, elderly women and a dozen black-suited men made up the overflow group thronging about the wide-open church doors. Inside I spied an unbelievably large crowd.

"Are the services always this crowded?" I asked.

"Always," he said. "And there are services throughout the entire day."

He shook hands with several of the men and in a moment, when word spread that I was an American visitor, the crowd immediately made way for me to go in.

"Come," said my friend as he started through the opening passageway.

I was about to follow him when I heard an excited voice call my name. Quickly a friendly hand touched mine and, turning, I heard a familiar voice exclaim in German, "How are you today?"

Anton and Olga stood before me, smiling and excited. Anton said, "You told us you were going to church. We thought it might be here."

I had mentioned my Sunday plans to them and since St. Nikolai was one of the largest of the five Russian Orthodox churches open in the city, there was no great mystery about the fact that they had found me. There was, however, a good question as to why they had come. Just to see me? Perhaps to discover why I wanted to attend the services? Or, I wondered, was the longing I had sensed in them— the longing for something that faith can give—strong enough to draw two young atheists almost inside church walls for the first time in their lives?

"Come along," I invited.

They shook their heads.

"It's not for us!" Olga said with a toss of her head.

"We'll be here when you're through," Anton assured me. "We'll wait."

My Sunday morning host viewed all this with surprise, then took my hand, and led me inside.

Two services were going on simultaneously in St. Nikolai, one upstairs where a second floor had been constructed to provide additional worship space, and one below in the church proper. It seemed to me that this unusual arrangement demonstrated genuine resourcefulness on the part of the church officials. In a city where churches are limited, the parishoners had actually made two churches out of one. Scaffolding against several pillars suggested that additional work was also under way.

My friend left me alone to worship as I wished. He was soon lost from my view in the tightly packed throng of standing worshipers. In contrast to Roman Catholic practices, the worshipers in the Russian Orthodox faith stand throughout the entire lengthy service. There are no pews in a Russian Orthodox church. It is considered an affront to the Lord to sit in His presence. There are other differences between Eastern Orthodoxy and Western Catholicism. Icons —pictures covered with metal and jewels except for the faces and hands—take the place of statues of the saints. They receive great veneration and the people bow to them and make the sign of the cross.

The sign of the cross in the Russian Church is made with the thumb and middle fingers joined together, touching the forehead first, then the breast, then the right shoulder and then the left. This act is accompanied by bending low from the hips. There are also special acts of reverence, called inclinations, which are made by prostrating oneself until the forehead touches the floor.

In place of the Roman Catholic altar, there is the iconostas, a magnificent series of icons extending from floor to ceiling. In the center of this are the sacred doors which, at the highest moment of worship—the sacramental act—are opened, revealing the inner sanctuary containing figures of the apostles or the figure of Christ on an icon or in stained glass.

I stood in crowded St. Nikolai church unobserved and unnoticed while myriads of candles and colored lamps burned before the icons, and the smell of incense rose from the acolytes' censers. The Mass was a symbolical representation of the life of Christ from the beginning of His ministry until His ascension, and the ritual which was being enacted by the regally vested elderly priest cast a spell upon us all.

Around me the emotionally possessed congregation of elderly women and a few men murmured prayers and made their signs of the cross. The stately ritual, the antiphonal chanting of two choirs, the sense of longing and of hope on the part of the people reminded me of services of many faiths I had attended in many parts of the world. But this was different because this was Russia. This was worship in the heart of the land where religion has been discredited, man's search belittled, and a people's faith strangled by ridicule and anti-religious campaigns.

As I scanned the crowd in vain for young people of college age, I wondered what Anton and Olga were thinking. They had never seen the inside of a church. They had never looked upon the sacred gates or felt the sense of relationship with God which these worshipers were experiencing. I had been told by my friend who brought me that it was here, in 1942, that Metropolitan Alexis preached during the Easter services when Leningrad was bombed by the Hitlerites. St. Nikolai itself was damaged and Alexis cried out against the sins of those who "dared to take as their banner the pagan swastika instead of the Cross of Christ."

Through the smoke of the censers I saw again the Museum of Religion. I saw Russia's defamation of the faith and I recalled the sculptured mother and child staggering beneath the cross. What would Alexis say about the sins of those who had taken up the hammer and sickle instead of the Cross? Round about me I felt the ageless quest for God, the Divine Force which has forever given strength to those who believe and new meaning in life to those who seek it.

I heard the chanting of the choirs invoking the plaintive plea of *"Gospodi, Gospodi pomilui."* (Lord, Lord, have mercy upon us.) I saw the worn and aged hands of the worshipers as they passed slips of paper upon which they had scribbled requests for prayer—passed them along from person to person until they reached the priest. I watched as he spread out these requests before him on a table and as he read them silently. I wondered whether faith can ever die.

Outside, young Russia was waiting. When they said, "We have never seen nor heard God," were they telling the truth? With what did they associate the good and the beautiful? How did they know what worship was like if they had never worshiped? What examples did they follow in developing virtuous habits? Who took the place of a Jesus in their lives? And if ever, in some inexplicable moment, they felt like praying, to whom or to what did they pray?

The crowd suddenly surged forward and I was carried along, forward to the magnet that drew the people. The priest held before him, upraised, a golden cross. One by one the faithful feverishly pressed their lips against it. Tears were in the eyes of many as they made the sign of the cross and bowed low, then raised their eyes and murmured, *"Gospodi, Gospodi pomilui!"*

I found a place beside a pillar where it was possible for me to wait and watch and close my eyes and pray in my own Protestant way. The chanting filled the church. The priest raised the cross again and again, then turned to open the sacred door. The people watched, to see the Christ within, to enter once more into the mystery of faith.

Was this a nation waiting, or was it just a remnant of a lost and simple-minded peasantry perpetuating an illusion, an illusion accounted dead and discarded by the enlightened proletariat? Once more I had to ask myself: is man religious by nature or isn't he? Can the religious impulse be sublimated into a non-religious ideology? Can a nation endure without a concept of God?

Russia was the riddle. Russia was the laboratory in which these questions were being tested and tried, and it seemed to me that every person had a part somewhere in the great experiment.

2. The Cross and the Sickle

O N THE FLIGHT FROM LENINGRAD TO
Kiev I thumbed through a batch of news clippings sent by
a friend in the States. Among them was the story of a U.S.
Air Force pilot who had survived fifty-four days in the
remote Sierras after his jet exploded. The pilot was quoted,
"My firm belief in God kept me going. I prayed so much
I don't think I'll ever stop praying."

I turned from the clipping to look down on the gigantic
panorama of Russian space, the country and the people
to whom Lenin said, "Our struggle is to eliminate the
social roots of religion."

A village below me was teeming with people. It passed,
and we flew over land sparsely settled. Far in the distance
was a cluster of buildings representing a collective farm.
Now a war-torn settlement appeared with gaunt smoke-
stacks defying the ruins and miles of road without a car
or sign of life. Then a huge barren carpet of land, waste-
land and steppes, as if waiting for some great decision.
Russia, endlessly big, three times the size of the United
States, had a big assignment, "Eliminate the social roots
of religion!"

A hand touched my arm. It was the very engaging and very bald-headed Russian who sat across from me in the plane, holding a very bald-headed youngster on his lap. Actually their heads were shaven, down to the skin. They had gotten on at Minsk. The moment Lorena saw them she was fascinated by the picture possibilities and by the tremendous affection between the two. They were both charmers and they knew it.

Earlier I had given the boy a stick of gum. Now the father was inquiring of me by means of gestures what it was for. He had been studying the wrapper and turning the gum over in his hands. I demonstrated that it should be chewed. The boy wanted to try it but the father was not so sure. On an airplane where Chiclets are unheard of and in a country where gum is practically unknown, Wrigley's was an oddity. The stewardess, whose English was as bad as my Russian and whose uniform was as out-of-press as my traveling suit, shuddered and said, "It is bad on teeth. It is not polite." She repeated this for the shaven-headed man. He laughed and agreed.

The stewardess noticed the American clippings on my lap and caught sight of the picture of the jet and the air force pilot. She picked up the clipping, read it laboriously and at length smiled, shook her head and handed it back.

For most Americans, the pilot's story was just another saga of faith to be added to a continually growing list. His resort to religion was characteristic of a deeply inbred tendency in most of us in the United States. We were always "turning to religion." Accounts of the power of prayer appeared frequently in our newspapers and magazines. We were always pulling on the side of faith. But this was Russia. Below me lay the land and rivers of a nation whose leaders knew no God, felt no need for God and hoped their people would eliminate the search for Him.

There was a time, in the days of the tsars, when 90 per cent of the Russian people belonged to a church, but, say the Communists, the people never got anywhere then. They never shared in the land or in industry. They were never permitted to raise their heads or speak their minds or *think*. Liberation, says the party, came not by faith in religion, but by faith in revolution. Only when the Bolsheviks broke the tsars and the church did "God" let His people go.

Now we were flying over wooded hills and winding valleys. Then a group of white-washed homes and a collective farm passed beneath the wing of our two-motored plane. Soon we caught sight of the Dnieper, one of the most beautiful rivers in all of Russia and beside it the lovely city of Kiev, capital of the Ukraine. Church domes rose upward among the tree-shaded streets and cathedral walls could be clearly seen. Kiev, I had been told, is the "Jerusalem of Russia." It was here that Christianity in Russia began.

We headed for the landing field. I searched for my seat belt, then remembered there wasn't any. There was part of one where Lorena sat, next to me, so she added it to the strap of her gadget bag and hung on. We came barnstorming down, the pilot electing to land next to the runway on the ground rather than on the black-top strip. Russian pilots never failed to give us a thrill and landings were generally unannounced. We were learning early in our trip that Soviet flying is safe, but full of surprises.

From the very start of our three-day stay in Kiev everything was pleasant. The weather was considerably warmer and brighter than in Leningrad. The people were more

37

colorfully dressed, their life noticeably easier and more relaxed. Kiev had a good, free feeling. Even the pigeons flew in and out of the unscreened windows in our fourth-floor room at the Intourist Hotel.

Intourist guides continued to serve our needs and answer our requests and extend us all the liberty we wished; so much so, that by now I had written off the complaints of friends back home who said they had been Intourist captives during their Russian trips. These friends, however, had traveled in the U.S.S.R. during the days of Stalin. Restrictions then were undoubtedly severe and the secret police apparently did make themselves offensive. The de-Stalinization was good for Russia and, come to think of it, so far I had not seen a single Stalin statue anywhere along the way.

There was however, one statue that fascinated me: the huge bronze figure of a man with a cross looming like a colossus high above the Dnieper. A hundred years ago this gigantic, sixty-two foot image was placed upon its pedestal, and today it still looks down upon the river as its undisputed conqueror. This is Prince Vladimir, monarch of Russia from 980 to 1015, a ruler so absolute that he divided his kingdom among his twelve sons.

Originally he was called Vladimir the Pagan. To gain the throne he killed his brother Yaropolk who had killed another brother, Oleg, before him. Vladimir celebrated his ascent to the throne by murdering a number of servants and killing a number of horses as an offering to Svarog, the Slavic god of gods. But shortly after his notorious sacrifice, Vladimir suddenly tired of killing and looked around for a religion which did not demand the shedding of blood.

38

It is said he sent his emissaries to many parts of the world to investigate the religions men lived by. They gave him a report on Islam and wondered whether that might appeal to him. It did not because Islam forbade its subjects to drink. Then they explained the influence and belief of Judaism. He rejected this because it opposed the eating of pork. So the emissaries told Vladimir about Christianity and he found nothing in the faith to conflict with his new way of life or interfere too much with his change of heart.

Furthermore, he liked Christianity because it was flourishing in Byzantium, the greatest power in the East. Vladimir's informers, in their appraisal of Byzantine Christianity, reported, "We went to Greece, and the Greeks led us to the edifices where they worship their God. When we arrived there we knew not whether we were in heaven or on earth. Never have we seen such splendor and beauty. We are at a loss to describe it. God dwells there among men and the services of the Greeks are fairer than the ceremonies of any other nation."

Vladimir was also advised that in the Byzantine empire the emperors dominated the church and the church dominated the people. It was different in Rome where western Christianity was flourishing. In Rome, Pope Gregory VII insisted that the Pope was mightier than the emperor, that the Pope was, in fact, appointed by God in an unbroken succession of popes from the time of Peter. Hence, of the two institutionalized expressions of Christianity, Byzantine or Roman, Vladimir much preferred the former.

He ordered his subjects to be baptized, some by persuasion, others by coercion. He issued proclamations: "There will be baptism in the river. Those who do not come will incur my displeasure." He demonstrated his good intentions by destroying the image of Svarog, the god of gods, and Perun, the god of thunder, and Vales, the god of cattle, and all the other Slavic gods and Norse deities. He replaced them with icons bearing the gentle face of the Virgin and the grieving, thorn-crowned Man from Galilee.

There had been pre-Vladimir attempts to bring Christianity to Russia. St. Andrew, the brother of Peter, preached, it is said, on the shores of the Dnieper shortly after the death of Christ. In 950, Princess Olga of the Russian aristocracy was baptized at Byzantium and founded a church at Kiev. The apostles to the Slavs, Cyril and Methodius, preached in nearby Moravia as early as 850, invented a Slavonic alphabet and translated the Bible.

But it remained for "Vladimir the Pagan" to make the faith official, to assign it to his subjects and to use it as an instrument of domination. It is Vladimir who stands on the hill and it is Vladimir the Christian whose hand clutches the shimmering cross. And that is how Christianity officially became the "holiest religion of the Russ."

The contrast between the coming of Christianity to Russia and the coming of the faith to America was sharp and clear as I talked with my Ukrainian guide near the statue. When I went to school I was taught that the early settlers came to our shores with the "Word of God in their hands and the fear of God in their hearts." I was assured that their first act was prayer, their first meeting one of Thanksgiving, their first service Holy Communion. Stamped on my mind were faith's milestones: the Pilgrims trudging to church, a communion service at Jamestown, Washington praying at Valley Forge. American religion, I was told, was gloriously interwoven with American history, and I felt we had done our Christian best, even by the redskins.

I was always proud of every historic mention of Religion, U.S.A.

When my Kiev guide, who was thirty-three, went to school, he learned about Religion, U.S.S.R. He was taught that the story of St. Andrew was fiction. He was warned that Princess Olga was a cunning witch, made worse, not better, by the Christian faith. He was taught that she accepted gifts of pigeons from her enemies, then tied firebrands to the pigeons' feet and let them fly back to burn up the towns. Cyril and Methodius were presented to him as good scholars, but bad agents of a foreign power. As for Prince Vladimir, he became a Christian because of political advantage. Historic truth assured my guide that Vladimir's twelve sons were the offspring of various wives, and the chronicles clearly stated that one of the sons, who became ruler only after much intrigue and fratricide, appointed and installed the first Russian-born Metropolitan of the Russian church.

Obviously, my guide's "milestones of faith" were startlingly unlike mine. History had given me something to live up to in the lives of America's men and the tradition of American events. Religion for me was the force that kept people free, that guided people right, that led people forward and upward in their dreams of a homeland and a nation. Religion for my Russian guide—and millions like him—was a conspiracy between tsars and patriarchs at the expense of the people, plotting between church and state in which the people were exploited, schemes among religionists and foreign powers in which the people were usually destroyed.

Young Russia knew religion as an evil; we Americans saw it as a blessing. They saw it as a weapon in the hands of the powerful; we thought of it as an element of restraint. They called it a rod in the hands of the rich and a whip in the hands of the priests. Small wonder that my guide concluded, "If this is religion, let us have none of it. If this is God, give me none of Him."

So I, with my trust in religion, and my guide with his distrust for it, decided to hold to our own impressions. Which we did. And we walked away together, leaving Vladimir standing on the hill to brood over the Dnieper. We left him there in the blazing sun to ponder, if he wished, what chance his ancient cross might have against the modern hammer and sickle.

What chance does it have? Just now my answer was, "None," for we were entering the torn and battered grounds of the Kiev-Pecherskaya monastery. War and time and the abandonment of religion had here worked together to turn one of Russia's holiest places into desolation. The Kiev-Pecherskaya Lavra, as it is called, has the excellent situation of a fortress over the Dnieper valley. Once the monks were trained here to kill those who tried to invade the land. The tsars taught the monks how to fight. The monks taught the tsars how to pray.

But Pecherskaya monastery was first and foremost a place for spiritual retreat. Here stood the great Cathedral of St. Sophia. Here St. Hilarion lived as a hermit, and a certain St. Anthony lived a life so pious that it "changed the hearts of the peasantry." Here St. Theodosius demonstrated the meaning of Christian austerity and here the great St. Nestor lived and died. Once it was the spiritual center of Russian Orthodoxy, foremost among 1800 monasteries which honeycombed the land. Today there are less than 50. Pecherskaya already seems more like a museum than a place for prayer.

A bearded monk poked aimlessly among the crushed and powdered stones of what was once a chapel. He stopped and looked up. High above him the vivid gold and red blaze of a fresco shimmered on a tottering wall. Once this was the hallowed interior of a great cathedral. Now it stands alone among the tangled mass of sacred rubbish.

Pecherskaya tugged at my heart. I saw what the monk saw—a fragment of the past without any plan or hope for restoration. The Communists want the wall to remain, want it to stand as it is, as long as it will. It is a symbol of what the German Luftwaffe wrought in one inexorable night. They left a campanile standing, also part of a chapel, part of St. Sophia and the frescoed wall. Actually, the work of a hundred years and the labor of ten thousand hands were turned to ruin and desolation between the hours of dusk and dawn.

An elderly French artisan sat in an improvised shack painstakingly restoring an ancient painting. He had his questions: "Where are the children of the men who created these murals? Where are the sons of the artists who made these icons? Where are the descendants of the architects who planned these walls and cupolas? No matter what the church may have been in the past, no matter how corrupt its leaders, the artists were inspired. They were in love with God. They are gone now. All gone. They no longer exist and they are not being reborn. Modern men know only the art of destruction. In that all men and all nations excel."

There are catacombs at Pecherskaya and, as is the case everywhere in the world, there are guided tours. I paid a modest fee, was handed a candle, and joined a small, expectant group which had gathered out of nowhere. Our guide for the underground excursion was a young post-revolutionist Russian who had long ago decisively settled the argument between the Cross and the sickle. To him this assignment was more than a tourist attraction; it was an opportunity to expose the heresies of the faith which once ruled Pecherskaya, and a chance to get in a few good licks for Communism's appraisal of religion. He could speak five languages: Russian, Ukrainian, English, German and French.

Our first descent, some ten steps down, took us past an aging, hooded monk, standing immobile as a mummy, holding a lighted taper clenched in both hands. The flicker of light struck his heavily bearded face. It touched his eyes, disclosing searchless wonder at the sight of people entering the sacred tunnels laughing and talking of spooks. He had probably seen and heard this many times, days on end, but he still found it amazing. He stood there, his brown habit blending into the damp niche. It was as though some strategist had set him thus, impaled him there for all to see how futile is God's cause, how weird and warped is custom, how out-of-date the simple-minded follower of Christ. It was as if someone had vengefully set him there and ordered, "Hold the candle until we tell you to let it go, stupid brother. Hold it there that all may see the last faint flicker of your dying faith."

The passageways are six feet high. They have been grubbed out of the earth, dug out of the rock and then smoothed over with layers of thick, dark clay. They are so narrow we had to always walk single file. Every few steps brought us to a crypt where coffins hold the shrouded bodies of the ancient Pecherskaya brotherhood.

Our candles permitted us to see the blackened hands and shriveled skulls beneath the glass-covered caskets. Then our guide explained in several languages how absurd it was for men to live and die in these self-appointed dungeons.

"Some people like to think," he announced, "that these bodies are miraculously preserved. Well, you can see for yourself. They are just like any other dead bodies. When the monastery became the property of the people, it was discovered there were quite a number of women buried along with the men. Since no women were supposed to have been allowed in Pecherskaya, you figure this out for yourself."

He resumed his march as though his words were gospel of a sort, but suddenly a Midwestern feminine voice from our group spoke up.

"Oh, just a moment now," it said indignantly. "The sisters could have been buried here out of respect. It doesn't follow that these people were immoral just because you think they were."

We stopped in our tracks at this unrehearsed inclusion in our tour. For a moment the tunnels were as silent as their dead. I lifted my candle to get a better look at the challenger. So did our guide. He turned as if to ask, "Who said that?" But before he had a chance to speak, the resourceful American voice went on, "I don't mean to say you haven't a right to your opinion. I just don't happen to agree with you."

She looked at him calmly, somewhat shyly, but her voice had been sharp just the same, sharp with a kind of petulance. She was in her thirties, a quiet-appearing, self-sufficient, pretty woman with a shoulder-strap purse and a camera and carrying her candle between her first and second fingers, palm up, just as we had been instructed to do. She had a print handkerchief tied around her auburn hair, a headcovering quickly put on for going to church.

"If you look at these things with suspicion," she was saying, "you can read all sorts of meanings into them."

"Very well," replied the guide in full recovery. "As I said, every person can figure out for himself and believe what seems right to him. So, now, watch your step, here we go down into another section."

We went down, judge and jury and the woman who had spoken in defense of the dead. Our guide hurried us past a grotto in which an old woman knelt with forehead touching the cobblestone floor. Around her huddled a small group of worshipers mumbling prayers and making the sign of the cross against their dark-clothed bodies.

The guide paused at a sarcophagus. He held his candle close to a picture above it and said, "Now here is a portrait of the fellow who lies here. You see, he is supposed to be a saint. Men became saints for many reasons. Most of the reasons are rather strange, like seeing visions or performing magic or fasting until they no longer cared to eat, or perhaps collecting more money than was expected of them. For in those days the church was very remunerative business. This poor fellow was made a saint for a different reason. He was sainted because he never spoke. You can see it written right here: 'He kept forever silent.' So, he is a saint."

He smiled and waited, candle in hand, to see whether anyone would care to challenge him. Someone did.

"I just don't think you're fair," said our defender of the faith. "Either you don't want to be fair or you know nothing about religious practices. This man wasn't a saint because he kept silent. He kept silent because he was a saint. You simply don't understand the life of religious people."

"I understand what it says here," retorted the guide. "It says, 'He kept forever silent.' There is his picture. There he lies, dead. But he is a saint. Do you know how powerful religion is? Just about as powerful as that little candle you're carrying."

He led us on. The girl said to me, "It really *isn't* fair. He shouldn't say those things. They aren't true. It isn't only what he says, it's the way he says it."

She was Roman Catholic and she loved her church with such a passion she had love to spare for the Russian Orthodox and the whole Eastern Rite which, she reminded me, "broke away from the Mother Church in 1058." She was sorry about that, the breaking away. The Great Schism had divided the Christian family, but Rome was absolutely in the right, she was sure. The separation of Christianity between East and West was due to more than just a cultural difference. The Eastern Church permitted itself to be dominated by the emperors and the tsars. It also refused to recognize the primacy of the Pope. It objected to the "filioque clause" which stated that the Holy Spirit descended not only from God the Father, but from the Son as well. The East, she maintained, had always been more concerned with theological argumentation than with living the Christian life. But despite her historical criticism, or because of it, she was mindful of the Russian saints and had a deep conviction that someday soon the whole Russian church would return to Roman Catholicism. She was always praying for the salvation of Russia; everyone in the Mother Church was praying for that.

When we stood before the picture of St. Nestor which adorned a dark corner in the catacombs, she inquired of the guide, "What do you think of him? Wasn't he one of Russia's great saints?"

"Correction, please," was the reply. "Nestor was one of our great chroniclers. That is admitted, but we must always be careful to separate history from mythology. We must differentiate between the qualities a man holds in one field and those he professes in another. Consider Tolstoy. Tolstoy was an able writer, but that is not to say he was a good philosopher."

At this moment singing was heard, choral singing enhanced by the dark, reverberating catacomb setting. It was evidently coming from the grotto where the women had been at worship. We paused instinctively and listened. Our Catholic spokesman, who in our minds had become quite an advocate for faith's cause, stood near me. Her eyes were ecstatic as if heaven had suddenly sprung to her defense.

"Well, come," commanded the guide. "We must be on our way. Our candles are burning out."

He led us on, past icons, coffins and shrines, past rectangular chambers in which an occasional worshiper knelt and prayed. Nevertheless we could not outdistance the singing. It echoed through the cloistered passages and trailed us until we reached the out-of-doors.

The guide was wrong about the candles. We had light to spare.

The Catholic woman was a schoolteacher from Nebraska whose convictions had been forged through years of study in a convent. She confided to me she had come to Russia to find out what was happening to religion, particularly Roman Catholic religion. Several weeks of unhindered inquiry had convinced her that the churches are indeed open in the U.S.S.R. and that Christianity has a chance to grow if the people want it to grow. Her feeling was that Russians are deeply religious but that the shock of persecution and early post-Revolution opposition have made the masses hesitant to affirm their faith even now. She had discovered many small, devout Roman Catholic congregations, had worshiped with them and had talked to the priests.

Her major interest now was in locating Uniat congregations. She felt "Uniatism" might be the answer to controversies that still existed between Catholicism and Orthodoxy. Uniats is the name applied to Christians who are in union with both the Russian and Roman churches. They retain the liturgy and forms of Orthodoxy, but acknowledge the primacy of the Pope and the Roman Catholic articles of faith. She was sure that somewhere in Communist Russia the Uniats were worshipping, even though many had been liquidated during the war as accused propagandists for Poland.

"God's true people will always rise again," she declared prophetically and repeated her conviction that the "Eastern Orthodox prodigals would one day return to their spiritual home in the west."

Now, of course, Eastern Orthodox churches do not think of themselves as prodigals. They are solemnly convinced that their church and not the Church of Rome is the true church. They believe their patriarchs to be the direct spiritual descendants of St. Peter, their liturgy to be God-inspired and their creeds and codes to be infallibly divine. Furthermore, it is the Russian Orthodox Church which accuses *Rome* of all sorts of heterodoxies. It lists among the "Latin errors" such things as baptizing by sprinkling instead of immersion, of advocating celibacy for the priesthood, of putting too much stress and fear into the teaching of purgatory, and too much emphasis on the primacy of the Pope; to say nothing about the heresy of eating eggs and cheese during Lent. Then there is also the Russian contention that Rome is in league with imperialism and an agent of capitalistic power.

"We find many admirable things about Roman Catholicism," a Russian Orthodox official said to me, "but the true church is not in the West, but in the East. When Christ comes again, he will come first not to Rome or New York or even Istanbul, but to Moscow. It has well been said, 'The Church of ancient Rome fell because of Apollinarian heresy. The second Rome, Constantinople, was hewn down by the axes of the Ishmaelites. But the third Rome, Moscow, the Holy Apostolic Church, shines through the entire world more brightly than the sun. Two Romes have fallen, but the third stands and no fourth can ever be.' "

I was sure he meant it, although it was becoming ever more difficult to break through what I felt was apprehension and restraint on the part of the clergy to share their true feelings about Russian religion. The weight of their opinion was always complimentary to the State. Never would they criticize the party, never would they challenge governmental policies.

To say the least, the Russian religious scene was deceptive. True, churches were open, but churches were also closed.

Freedom of religion was a reality. The Constitution provided it. But it also provided freedom to disseminate anti-religious propaganda.

It was quite correct to say there was a separation of church and state, but the state owned the church properties, and Communist party members were not allowed to belong to a religious organization.

Teaching of religion was permitted, but it was also strictly limited. No religious teaching was allowed in the case of children under eighteen in groups of more than three.

It was true that the people were free to avail themselves of the churches' ceremonies, but informed atheism had grown so powerful psychologically that many worshipers were shamed into staying away from the church. For example, "Marriages," says Communist law, "*must* be solemnized by the state and *may* be solemnized in the church." Actually only 10 per cent of marriages in Russia today are officiated over by a clergyman.

"Anyone in Russia can find a place to worship if he looks for it," I was told. But 80 per cent of the people had been persuaded not to look.

To pursue these matters further, I returned one evening to Pecherskaya monastery to see what a center of Russian Orthodoxy would be like at vesper time, to try to find out for myself whether or not a spiritual night had fallen over it and to visit, if possible, the monks' living quarters and speak with some of the men.

Unable to secure an interpreter, I persuaded a friendly taxi driver to take me out to the grounds. At first he hesitated. I offered to tip him. This offended him so he decided to take me to prove that his reluctance had absolutely nothing to do with a tip.

Pecherskaya Lavra was deserted when we arrived, but at the ghostly entrance to the catacombs a bearded, brown-cowled monk stood with hands hidden in his sleeves. I made myself understood sufficiently for him to lead me to a side gate which led to the monastery proper. Then he misunderstood me and left me standing there. I walked to the rear entrance and proceeded down a darkening corridor which led to the sleeping quarters. I thought that was where it led, but I was stopped by a gentle, muffled voice questioning in soft, sing-song Ukrainian tones, "Where are you going, brother, where are you going?"

The words were repeated over and over, but I saw no one. Then, after a moment, I spied an aged monk seated in a dark corner on a bench. His hands rested on a walking stick. He rocked slowly back and forth and asked, "Where are you going, brother?" His forehead was nestled on his hands and I could not see his face.

I tried to ask in Russian, "Where do I find the abbot?"

He did not look up.

I asked the question in English, taking a few steps in his direction. He raised his head. His beard was closely cropped; his heavy hair was as dark as the corner in which he sat. And his eyes were blind.

His face was one of the most serene and gentle I have ever seen. He was smiling and it was a look of extreme compassion and simple questioning. Turning slightly in my direction he asked again, "Where are you going, brother, where are you going?" The expression on his face was one of quiet triumph, as if to say, "I could tell by the sound of your steps that you are not one of us. You are a stranger. I know. Do not think that because I am blind, I cannot see."

Since there was nothing I could say or do, I walked away. But I felt I would never forget the blind gatekeeper at Pecherskaya Lavra. The question he had asked me was the question I wanted to ask Russia, "Where are you going?" For it seemed to me that the sound of its step was different from that of any nation in the world. How or why, I could not tell, unless I related it to my estimate of religion's meaning in the life of man.

A vague contrast between people who believe in God and those who do not struck me forcibly as I turned from the blind and gentle monk. The contrast had to do with the supreme worth of the soul or, at any rate, the supreme worth of the individual. Communism, it seemed to me, lacked not only the comprehension or even the good guess about the nature of God, it even lacked a comprehension and a guess about the true nature of man. There is, I told myself, definitely a difference between those who live by the hammer and sickle and those who live by the Cross; even a blind man in the dark knows that.

My taxi driver had come to look for me. He was not worried, but he wanted to remind me there was a charge for waiting. He did not mind waiting, either. He just wanted to advise me so that we would understand each other when it came time to settle up.

I assured him this was kind of him and asked if he would go to the chapel with me. He smiled and shook his head. Did I know where the chapel was? It was over there where several beggars sat hopelessly in the dirt outside the door. But beyond them, in the dusky interior, white-scarved women stood with folded hands facing the censer-swinging priests.

A group of bearded monks were crowded into a choir stall in the left transept. Other monks stood in prayer stalls at the right. The congregation consisted of perhaps a hundred peasant women, a half a dozen men and a few youths.

The gold-covered iconostas extended from floor to ceiling and in the dimly candle-lighted room the ancient colors sent out shafts of light. The rising smoke from the silver censers, the continually bowing worshipers formed the setting for a lengthy Scripture reading intoned in the old Slavonic language by a bearded monk. I understood not a word of it, but it was interesting to conjecture that words like these had been recited here uninterruptedly for nearly a thousand years.

Pecherskaya Lavra has seen the invasion and plunder of more than twenty wars. The monastery was used as a fortress during the Mongol and Tartar invasions. The catacombs were air-raid shelters during World War II. Hitler gave the Nazis orders to subvert the Orthodox Churches or destroy them. He had already set up a school in Breslau to train men to take over the Russian Church after the Nazis conquered the land. They never conquered it. They never stilled the chanting at Pecherskaya, chanting unbelievably beautiful, which I was hearing now. No outside power had ever defeated the church. Could the Communistic power within Russia defeat it?

I listened to the chanting and I seemed to hear the priest say to me again, "The future of the church is up to the people."

I remembered how Christians in America had thrilled when, at the height of the Nazi invasion of Russia, Patriarch

Sergius of the Russian Orthodox faith said to Hitler, "You have deprived your people of the freedom of religion against their will. You can never do it to us. The Church of Christ gives its blessing to our Orthodox people. The Lord will grant us victory."

In those days, we in the United States were praying for victory along with the Russian people. England was praying. The Buddhists were praying. The Jews and the Moslems were praying. In those days a bishop of the Armenian Church said in a sermon: "It is a million times happier and more desirable to live in a godless land of Soviets than in the nest of those venomous snakes and cannibals, the Fascists. Fascism is an evil spirit, and Hitler will not find absolution either on earth or in heaven. Cursed be the cannibal. May God punish the viper in the fires of hell!"

As I thought of this, the struggle between the Cross and the hammer and sickle became ever more confusing. For by now perhaps God had punished Hitler and the fires of hell had punished him. By now England and the Buddhists and the Jews and the Moslems were no longer praying for Russia. And we were not praying for Russia, with the exception perhaps of the Blue Army of Roman Catholicism.

And where is the Russian Church that helped win the war? The Church that Patriarch Sergius talked about? Is it to be found in a hundred white-scarved women and a dozen bearded men in Russia's famous monastery at Pecherskaya in Kiev? I warned myself that this should be religious research and not religious sentimentality. I looked at the iconostas and asked myself the question the old French artisan asked, "Where are the children of these men?"

I closed my eyes and listened to the chanting. I wished that every Protestant and every Catholic and every person, no matter what he is or whether he is anything at all, could hear it. I said to myself, "Perhaps true religion is something no one even talks about. Maybe it is like music and love and beauty and that is all there is to it." And I thought what a much better place the world would be if everyone just loved God and never even spoke about Him to anyone, just loved Him and spoke to Him and let it go at that.

The service continued and the people crossed themselves and bowed whenever they heard the words, "Lord have mercy."

When it was over and I started in the direction of the cab, I met a man who spoke German and French and Ukrainian and Russian. He was a Russian officer and he happened to be in Kiev and he happened to be at the monastery. And there were three monks who tarried in the cloistered walk and through the kindness of the officer interpreter, I asked them, "How strong is the church in Russia?"

One replied, "You cannot measure spiritual strength."

"How many churches are there?"

"Thousands of churches. There are churches everywhere."

"Do you enjoy complete freedom of worship?" I asked.

"Of course. Why not?"

"How many monks are here?"

"About one hundred."

"Are there any young men?"

"There are some."

"How many?"

"Perhaps ten or twenty."

"What do you feel you are accomplishing?"

"We are God's servants. We are doing His will."

"Does God's will ever conflict with the will of the state?" I asked. "The state is atheistic. It does not recognize God. Isn't this a conflict with your belief?"

"The Scripture commands the church to recognize and obey the secular powers. That is our view."

"So you are subservient to the state?"

"No. There is a separation of church and state."

"Say that Russia engages in war. Would you sanction it even if it were an aggressive war?"

"Russia has never been guilty of an aggressive war. It does not want war. It wants peace."

"If Russia should be invaded, would you fight?"

"Of course."

"Even if the invaders were Christians?"

"We would. I do not understand how a Christian could consent to be an invader."

"Are Russian people particularly religious?"

"Russian people have always been religious."

"Do you think your leaders are spiritual people?"

"It is not for us to judge who is spiritual and who is not. They do not judge me; we do not judge them. They are spiritually minded."

"Which will triumph in Russia, the Cross or the hammer and sickle?"

"Is there a conflict?" I was asked.

"Of course there is a conflict! Lenin said the search for God should be given up? Isn't this a conflict?"

"The teaching of Lenin is a deep study, much deeper than most people realize."

"Is the Communist an enemy of religion?"

"Freedom of religion also implies freedom of non-religious belief. Our churches here are free and our churches are open."

"Does not the state own and control the churches?"

"The people own and control them. We are the people."

This kind of circular discussion went on and on. I could not break through the official opinion. I was frequently referred to the abbot, but he was out of town and that got us nowhere. Apparently the monks wanted nothing more than to convince me and my interpreter that the government was a friend of the church and a supporter of the faith. I might feel they had a different set of opinions and a different life behind their propagandism, but how right was I? Furthermore, was I not continually comparing religion in the U.S.S.R. with religion in the U.S.A.? It cannot be compared, I told myself. It need not be compared. After all, all I wanted was to find out whether belief in God is necessary in the life of a people.

But, whereas we in America have access to spiritual life and thought by way of hundreds of denominational periodicals, the Russian church is confronted with a ban on the publication and distribution of religious literature. Eastern churchmen no doubt have things to say, but no printed medium is allowed them. The lines of communication, as far as freedom of the religious press is concerned, are definitely down.

And a monk said, "For those who believe God is necessary, He is necessary. But in Russia, as in all countries, there are many who do not believe."

One of the monks lingered after the others and the interpreter had gone. His face was prison pale. He looked as if he had been struggling forever against an inner fear. He had offered no comment during our interview and why he stayed now, I did not know, for we had no common language in which we could communicate. He stood there, a bearded man of perhaps forty-five, looking at me with critical quizzing eyes.

He put his cowl over his head and said something which I could not understand. From his tone and his earnestness he seemed to be thanking me for having come.

I wondered what I could give him as a remembrance. The only thing I had was the inevitable Lincoln penny. A Lincoln penny or a ball-point pen! Every Russian who has ever met an American has a ball-point pen. Everyone I met would probably have a shiny Lincoln penny. We Americans are such insatiable givers. . . .

He settled the question for me by extending his hand and then covering my hand with both of his.

There is something a person feels that needs no language. Something universal. It asks for nothing, desires nothing, expects nothing. No political curtain, no sectarian wall, no ideological boundary, no lack of communication can confine it. Wherever it is found, God is found. It may be that it comes closer to a discovery of God than many things we know.

What can you read in the eyes of a monk? How far should one let his imagination carry him? Would this man return to his cell, wondering how much he could have told me? Would he say, "We told the stranger the truth, but he does not believe us?" Or, "We gave him the impression we are free, but actually we are not. There is a constraint upon us and we must weigh everything we do and say. There is something here we would like to escape from, but we do not know how. We say we have faith, but we have not enough faith to free ourselves."

Did he want to say that there is no hope for religion in Russia and tell me perhaps that I was right in my feeling that religion is actually as dead as the tsars and the Cross is no match for the hammer and sickle? Or did he want to remind me that he, too, often felt that faith was moving in the people as a subterranean force—rising nearer the surface day by day?

It was dark as I walked through the cloistered corridor back to where my driver sat dozing at the wheel. He laughed wonderingly at the time I had consumed in the old monastery where there was really nothing to be seen any more. It used to be a beautiful place before the days of Hitler.

We climbed the graveled hill and returned to the pleasant streets of Kiev, streets that seemed always gay, especially at night with the many young people, and the women selling bouquets on the street corners, and the neon lights and the cinema marquees making it look almost like a city in America.

My driver took me to the hotel and I paid him. He handed back my tip with a warning smile. Shaking his finger in pretended offense, he made me understand I was not to impress him with the mock generosity of the capitalistic system! After all, he had only done his duty. A good feeling, he assured me, is better than a few extra rubles any day.

3. Faith Is for the Free

IN KHARKOV a towering cupola caught my eye the moment I arrived at the Intourist Hotel. I was told it was the cathedral on the hill. No sooner had I checked in than I thought I would sally forth to visit it and also to catch the town's vibrations.

Kharkov, third largest city in the Soviet Union, is sprawling and wide with open spaces where the Nazis bombed and bled the earth in search of *Lebensraum*. They held Kharkov enslaved for two years, fully expecting to stay forever.

The cathedral on the hill is a brave and beckoning church. It stands as if it had been appointed to guard the canal and the city, the new city and the old which is being rebuilt. It looks over the homes which can never be rebuilt because the householders died there, shaking their fists against the skies.

And now the church stood there like God mourning over his people. I went up to pay my respects. To go, as it were, to the house of God in a godless land.

Lorena went with me for pictures. We drew near the

door, the main door that ordinarily leads to the nave, and I saw an iron bar across the entrance and an iron lock holding the bar in place like a mailed fist. Above the door a number of used boards had been roughly fixed as if to cover the spot where an icon had been ripped off. And as we stood there and as the people went by, I wondered what greater insult to religion, what grimmer reminder of religion's hopelessness than a lock that showed.

I went around to a side door and, lo and behold, it was open. Only it did not look like a church door. It looked more like a factory entrance, with a ramp and worn planks of the kind that heavy carts move over, wearing grooves and splintering the wood.

It was quite dark inside the doorway, though it was mid-afternoon. The narrow, boarded-up walls, forming a corridor, were damp and dingy, almost like the catacombs. A man came toward me, asked sharply where I was going, then passed by without waiting for an answer.

I had no answer anyway. I was going to church. I was visiting the brave cathedral whose head is held high above the city.

When I got to the foyer, I heard machinery, like factory machinery, faintly pounding a rhythmic tattoo that echoed upon the walls and spun a crazy chanting sound overhead. It was dark, but in a moment a door swung open, an inside door, and a heavy push-cart rolled out, guided by a workman. The cart was piled high with heavy boxes and behind this scene, in the nave of the cathedral from which the workman had come, were other boxes and cartons and barrels and supplies, stored against the icons and the pillars, while workmen moved them into place or out of place as though the surroundings had never been a church at all.

Several men had caught sight of me and by the time the cart had moved away, they had gathered around me demanding to know what I was doing in the factory, where I had come from, what I meant by walking in and whether no one had stopped me at the door. All the while the litany of the machines rattled on and when a workman opened a side door, I caught sight of rows of sewing machines with their operators bent intently over them. All of this was taking place in what was once a transept and, further on, in what might have been the sacristy.

Now I was being hurried out. It was not that the men did not want me to see how a cathedral can be adapted to a garment plant, or that I might not understand how, in the people's republic, work is worship. I simply needed a permit, which was reasonable enough. And I was told, if I was looking for a church, I would have no trouble finding one. For, they assured me, churches are open in Kharkov. So I walked out, away from the haunted voices of the machines and the sight of shipping boxes piled against the icons and images of saints.

I started back to the hotel through a park which, a man told me, was really not a park but a memorial.

"Before the war," he explained, "a large department store stood here. It was bombed by the Hitlerites. So many people were killed, it was decided to convert the area into a place where people can rest and reflect. You will see many memorials like this in Russia. Some will be even larger than this. Kharkov never really died. Cities like this do not die."

And I looked up once more to the cathedral on the hill, watching over the city.

It is easy to romanticize American faith when you

are in Russia. You think about our city churches and our country chapels and our people dressed in their Sunday best. Faith, you tell yourself, is for the free. You remember your own custom of church-going and how the day was different and enriched because you had been to the services. Literally speaking, Russia does not have a Sabbath as far as Communism is concerned.

But while you are romanticizing you also begin to wonder just what religion implies and what it is supposed to do. When you think about this, American religion runs through your mind, all the way from high-powered evangelism, which saves your soul, to positive thinking, which saves your reputation. When you have thought about all of that you look around you in a Russian city, like Kharkov, for example, and you meet the people, and you find that here where atheism is more than a term, where it is a way of life, people are courteous, hospitable and kind, just as they are back home.

You reach a conclusion something like this: in the light of Russia, we self-professed Christians ought to live out our faith more than we do. We should be more willing to demonstrate what we have in the way of a usable, workable, livable knowledge of God. Our faith should show up better than it does.

And when you have finished with this sort of preaching, you look once more at the cathedral on the hill, and you have a feeling that it could never stand forgotten in the U.S.A. You suddenly conclude with a feeling of joy and pride that variegated as our religious pattern is, having in it everything from make-believe to miracles, it is the life stream of our nation. The world will never understand our generosity, believe our humanitarianism or trust our motives until it grasps the simple nature of our faith. We are naive and childlike when it comes to religion, but it may be that because of this we often catch what we feel to be a fleeting glimpse of the kingdom of God. At any rate, we conclude, and no doubt rightly so, that we are what we are because of our tradition of faith.

The workmen were right, of course, about open churches in Kharkov. I found four of them. One, the Cathedral of the Assumption, three blocks from the hotel, would inspire worship in anyone whether or not he agreed with Russian Orthodoxy or even if he professed no formal faith at all.

It was a large, magnificent place of alternating maroon and yellow bricks giving the great domed structure a kind of tapestried effect. The dome and four cupolas were dwarfed by a bell tower which rose like a rocket, bearing majestically toward the sky its huge golden cross. An iron fence surrounded the triangular plot where the cathedral stood.

I had an appointment here one morning with one of the three priests, and my interpreter was to meet me outside the doors. I got there early and went on inside. The towering walls and pillars were arrestingly beautiful. The icons covering them were works of art. Traditional scenes from the life of Christ, portrayals of prophetic portions of Scripture, pictures of Russian patriarchs covered the arches and adorned the interior of the dome. The altars were alabaster white and above the sacred doors leading to the inner sacristy was a breathtaking painting of the Last Supper. Throughout the cathedral the beauty was so symphonic and rich one would have expected that here, more than in many another church, one would surely find the

Russian proletariat. Yet I found only a small group of peasants, elderly women who came and went, buying a taper or a sacred wafer at the counter in the front transept and getting their souls in order without benefit of a priest.

They were gentle, patient worshipers, very devout. Their faces showed much suffering and hardship, but as they stood motionless in thoughtful worship, making the sign of the cross, they apparently found something in these lavish surroundings that was precious and sustaining for their lives.

There was an old lady in black seated at a table in the dark of the transept near the door. She was an ageless nun laboriously writing in a book. Whenever I passed her in the shadows, I glanced at her because she herself looked almost like an icon. The touch of white beneath her black bonnet was a halo and her round, red face was as peaceful as a saint's. She scanned the pages of her book half over her glasses, and whatever she was writing must have been important, for she would write a while, read it slowly, then dip her long pen into the inkwell and write some more. Once when I passed her, she looked up. Her eyes met mine and I tried to phrase a question to inquire what she was writing. She peered at me over her spectacles. Her face lighted with a smile and before I could speak, she said with warmth and feeling, *"Slava Bogu."*

That was the first time anyone in Russia had said, "Praise the Lord," to me, and the way it was said did more for me than all my morning prayers and all my morning thoughts, and made me feel a good deal better about the Communists who had taken over the temple on the hill. Here, at least, people were free to say, "Praise the Lord." The smile accompanying the words, the twinkle in the old woman's eyes seemed to say, "Even a stranger must know the meaning of *Slava Bogu.*" She dipped her pen into the inkwell, touched the penholder to her lips and resumed her writing.

I felt as if I had glimpsed into the inner heart of a Russian worshiper, and not one worshiper only, but perhaps the hearts of many to whom the age-old greeting of *Slava Bogu* still had meaning. Did it lie so closely beneath the Russian consciousness that it needed only an understanding glance to call it forth? Was religion day-by-day really rising like the priest's "subterranean stream"? Could it be that people here in the U.S.S.R. actually loved God and held Him more precious than anyone realized? Did acquiescence to the state keep them from the services and was submission to atheistic ideology only a matter of expediency? Were people seeking God without even the church realizing it or the government knowing about it or a man's own neighbor being aware of it? In Stalin's day everyone spied upon everyone else, and people learned to live their real lives in the dark. Could it be that they were still being elusive and noncommittal about religion even now?

Such thoughts were, of course, mere speculations. And when I stopped to analyze them, all I could conclude was that they had been inspired by an old woman with a saintly face writing in a book, who did nothing more than greet me with "*Slava Bogu.*"

I went outside and found my interpreter waiting. She was in her mid-twenties and there was no need to ask whether she even attended religious services. I was sure she did not, but I asked her just the same. And she said, "No."

From the start I knew that she would be one of my very best interpreters. Not only an outstanding linguist, she also had a tremendous feeling and concern for people. Like all Russians of her generation, at least all whom I had met, she was an advocate of the socialistic point of view and believed that her country had made its greatest strides since the advent of Communism.

She was an attractive, dark-haired, dark-eyed girl in a neatly tailored dress which showed considerably more style than any I had noticed in shop windows. The dress was as modest as its wearer and there was no pretense about her. She wore make-up sparingly, had beautifully manicured hands, and even her shoes, open-toed, were far better than any I had seen for sale in Russian stores. Most of all, she gave the impression of being a resourceful, strong-charactered person with considerable poise and capability.

Her given name was Vera. She managed a small gift counter in the hotel and helped out as interpreter and guide for Intourist whenever needed. At the present time several tourist groups were in town—Czechs and East Germans—so she had been assigned to me. She was interested, she said, because my field was religion and that was something she knew very little about.

"What do you want to ask the priest?" she inquired.

I explained that I was interested in finding out about the state of religion, whether the church was gaining or losing ground, what people believed and whether Russia was actually as atheistic as its leaders claimed or could ever become as atheistic as its leaders wanted it to be.

"We can ask the priest all these things," she answered

confidently. "We can ask him any questions you like. I am sure he will be glad to tell you."

"Have you ever met him?"

"Oh, no. I have never even been inside the church."

"Lived here all your life," I reminded her with a laugh, "and never been inside the cathedral, not even to see what it looks like?"

"You've been here only a few days but you've seen more than I," she replied.

"Haven't you ever wanted to go into a church out of sheer curiosity?"

She was surprised at my question. "Why should I have curiosity? So I can tell tourists what it is like?"

"That might be one good reason."

"Few tourists ask to go to church," she said.

I inquired about her parents, whether they belonged to a church. She told me her father and two brothers were war casualties. Her brothers were killed defending Kharkov. Her father died as a result of the war. No, they had not belonged to a church.

"As for Mother," she said reflectively, "Mother used to go to church. I remember when I was a schoolgirl, she used to go to the service."

"Did she never ask you to go with her?"

"No. Now let me think. No, she didn't. You see, she knew that I was getting the necessary training in school."

"What kind of training?"

"In how to live. Moral training, I suppose you'd call it. I do remember that Mother used to pray. I remember how she made the sign of the cross. I always thought that was quite interesting, though I never really understood it."

69

"She doesn't belong to church now or go to church any more?"

"No. All of this was years ago."

"Before the war?"

"Before the war."

"Did the war dissuade your mother from going to church?"

"What do you mean?"

"Did the war destroy your mother's faith in God?"

"I really don't know. You see, when you say 'God' and ask about God, I really do not know what you mean. The war destroyed many things. I suppose it could destroy what you call 'faith,' too. But as for Mother, she just gradually stopped saying her prayers and making the sign of the cross. She has not done any of that for years. If she had any reason for stopping, I do not know about it. We do not discuss such things."

"But tell me, do you ever have a consciousness of God? Do you ever have an insight or feeling or sense of identity with God? Or, if the term 'God' is unacceptable, let's say a sense of Something or Someone Unseen, a Presence—"

"I really never analyze things that way or think in such terms. Should I?"

"Well, people have been thinking about such things for some time."

She laughed quietly. "Am I so different from anyone else? I don't think so. Some people feel the need for religion, others do not. I do not. I have no religious curiosity. Maybe I should have. Do you think I should?"

"Well," I said, "if you did have you might be able to tell an inquiring tourist about it."

70

"But I haven't. So, shall we go in and see what the priest has to say?"

I often thought I would like to take a Russian visitor into one of our American churches, but what more novel experience could I ask than to take a Russian into her own church for the first time?

We went inside. For a moment the full beauty of the setting caught my companion off guard. Her eyes swept over the scene, fell for an instant upon the group of women gathered in front of an altar and then rested upon the priest just entering the sacred doors with slow, contemplative steps. He was a tall, graying man, clean shaven; a benign, gentle-faced man whose alert eyes spied us with something of a flash. He approached with slightly bowed head, absently fingering the gold cross dangling against his long brown robe. There was nothing posed about him. In fact, he appeared to be a rather sad man whose office had endowed him with patience. A woman nearby hurried forward when she saw him. He tried to restrain her, but she took his hand in both of hers, bent low, kissed his hand and then, when he touched her head, she remained standing there, weeping for sheer joy, it seemed to me, at having had so great a privilege. Several other worshipers surged forward, but the priest lifted a hand and they waited. Then he came to where we stood.

Vera introduced herself and me, explaining why I had come and where I had come from. He welcomed us graciously and said two other priests would join us in a moment. Then he asked us to follow him. We walked past the old woman who was writing and who did not look up, past the pillars and the icons until we came to a dais where a layman arranged chairs and brought in a small writing table.

Here we sat with a view of the nave and the worshipers, though we were far enough removed to be quite alone. The morning light sparkled through the colored finger-like windows. The icons glistened. A bearded priest, swinging a silver censer on a chain, moved through the church, spreading a mist of thin smoke over the scene. The musical clank of the censer echoed in the church. The smell of incense drifted over to us.

Vera smiled as if to admit there was a certain enchantment here, but I suspected she felt it was not necessarily a desirable enchantment. It was, rather, a certain magic which should not be trusted too far. Things of this kind, she may have been thinking, play upon the emotions, upon one's sentimentality; there is a certain theatricalism about them, so let us not trust them too far.

Then she said, "So, shall we begin our interview?"

Two other priests had joined us. They were men in their mid-forties, very interested and courteous throughout a meeting which continued for more than an hour, a meeting which can be summed up with one conclusive opinion: the clergy of the Russian Orthodox Church are not prepared to say one word against the government. They may be speaking either from the basis of facts or fear. I could not tell which. Perhaps they have no grievances against the government, or perhaps they feel themselves in complete subjection to the party bosses. It may be they fear the power the Kremlin wields. Whatever it is, the impression given was the same I had found everywhere along my trip, "The churches are open. The future of religion is up to the people."

A question, "Is your church completely free or is it subject to domination by the Communist party?" was answered, "We are, of course, entirely free. We have been free ever since the Soviet order was established."

"Are you free to propagate the faith?"

"Why shouldn't we be? No one hinders us."

"Haven't restrictions been placed on the church and on your educational system and on your entire program?"

"There have been changes, of course, but we need not view changes as restrictions."

"Weren't there many persecutions of church leaders after the Revolution and are there not likely to be persecutions again if the church does not follow the restrictions the state has placed upon you?"

"There have been instances of arrest among religious leaders, but these were not the result of religious infractions. Some were found guilty of being enemies of the Soviet order. That is another matter. The decree of 1918 forms the basis for church and state relationship."

"Didn't the church object to this decree and resist it?"

"That history is long and involved," said one of the priests with a sigh.

I thought about the statement and the way it was said after our interview was over and long after Vera had casually shrugged off any new knowledge of religion merely as part of general knowledge. Surely, she contended, there is nothing mysterious or miraculous about religion. It can all be explained as man's struggle against man. Why bring the "gods" into it? Such an approach, she observed, could only confuse the picture and blind us to reality.

She was, of course, thinking in terms of Russian religion, just as my guide had in Kiev. But it was exactly this, the historical reality of religion in Russia, which could give us our best understanding both of contemporary Russian faith and the Communist attitude.

The early Russians whom Vladimir forced to become Christians back in the tenth century never actually gave up their pagan practices. They never became Christians in the western Protestant sense of the term. The church knew it and the priests knew it. They knew that in the mind of the peasant, Christianity was an attempted substitute for pagan worship. Priests took the places of the gods, icons were substituted for charms, sacraments replaced the fetishes, and when the people were called upon to give and suffer for the propagation of the faith, it was just another form of sacrifice of the kind once demanded by Svarog and Parun.

Religion was nationalized from the time of Vladimir up to the very hour of the 1917 Revolution. There was no separating church and state just as there was no separating paganism from Christianity. The church taught respect for the emperor or tsar despite his often dubious character. It insisted that poverty and ignorance were part of the divine order, and the main function of the church was to perpetuate itself regardless of the concessions it might have to make.

Compared with Roman Catholicism, Russian Orthodoxy produced few great philosophers and even fewer saints. It had neither the theological depths nor the dogmatic wisdom of the western church, but neither did it have a Reformation. It was never confronted by a Luther or a Calvin, a Zwingli or a Knox. It was born of opportunity and nurtured on compromise, and no one ever had the courage to nail a thesis to its door.

But it had one insistently stubborn conviction: it believed itself to be the true church of Christ and imagined itself divinely protected against any force from within or without. It concluded that God miraculously protected it against the abortive revolution of 1905. It closed its ears to cries for reform. It ridiculed the intrusion of Marxist doctrines which crept into Russia as part of the process of Westernization. Throughout the pre-revolutionary period there were struggles for power between the Orthodox hierarchy and schismatic religious groups. The church was dissolute and divided, and ridiculed the possibility of a Bolshevik *coup d'état*. It boasted of being the true church of Christ and clung to this belief even when it awoke in 1917 and found the godless Bolsheviki in power.

The gap between the Church of the tsars, which was arrogant, secularistic, and superstitious, and the Russian Church of today, confused, defensive, and captive, is a wide gap. Priests I interviewed always gave me the impression that they were secretly and hopefully waiting for a prophetic voice and a powerful hand to lead them out of the confusion and disillusionment of a thousand years.

This was also the feeling I had about Protestantism in Russia. Intourist had graciously arranged a hotel room meeting for me with an Evangelical-Baptist pastor in Kharkov. The Baptists came to Russia nearly a hundred years ago when a Russian was converted to the Baptist faith in Germany and returned to his homeland as a missionary. This was contrary to the laws at the time which forbade proselytizing. He carried on his work "underground," however, supported by Baptist groups in England and America.

The Kharkov pastor was a tall, lean, middle-aged man,

unpretentious and unclerical in a brown business suit. He was all for talking religion and eager to tell me about his congregation of nearly a thousand souls who were just now remodeling their church and looking forward to continuing growth in membership. The growth was slow, to be sure, and religion could not be measured by the kind of enthusiasm we enjoyed in the United States, but he was optimistic about the future. "The church," he said, "is on its own and what it will do depends upon the church."

Vera, who was again my interpreter during this hotel interview, asked me if that made sense. I said it did and she said, "I'm glad," for evidently the statement had no meaning for her. She rarely commented on anything that was said in these interviews and never editorialized, not even when the minister in speaking of "Christian virtues," suddenly said, "No one who smokes can possibly belong to my church." I told him this was not the case in most churches in America. "Ah!" he exclaimed, "I know, I know. But it should be!"

I said I was surprised to hear him emphasize this rather than such issues as the position of the church in the world, its attitude on war, its importance as an instrument of world brotherhood. "Those things are vital, of course," he declared. "But the individual must first give evidence of his faith by living the Christian life."

"But," I had to say, "the moral life which you stress is one which Communism also stresses, apart from any religious or Christian emphasis. Don't you think people can be morally good outside of the church?"

"They can," he replied. "The state wants its young people, all of its people, to be good people. Of course, this is true. So, we can work together on this, can't we?"

76

"Can you work together in other fields? Are there no ideological conflicts between your church and the state?"

"We are entirely free," he said. I again received the stock answers to all of my questions: the church is open, the people are free to worship, there is no conflict between religion and the state. He came back to his moral emphasis at every opportunity, going so far as to say that the Bible specifically forbids smoking.

I did not ask him to put his hands on the text that proved it.

"Here is my interpreter," I said. "She doesn't smoke. She is a highly moral person. She represents a generation that has never been inside a church, yet she impresses me as being fully as 'moral' as young people who go to church."

"I have no doubt," he agreed. "Russian young people are very good." To which he added, "And it is good that they are."

"So, what is the purpose of the church? What is its function?"

"There is the matter of salvation," he said, after a moment.

"You mean that people who do not belong to church will not be saved; that is, go to heaven?"

He gave the question thought and said, "No one knows what God does in these matters or how God judges people. But there is a special duty upon us who believe in salvation through the Church and the Word. There is a duty upon us to be loyal to His church."

"And loyal to the state? Even if the state is anti-church?"

"The state is not antichurch. The church is free and

separated from the state. The Scripture tells us to give to Caesar that which is Caesar's."

He returned to the subject of morals and asked me to tell him a bit more about religion and morals in the United States. Which I did. This was neither easy nor simple, especially since my listener shook his head continually and murmured audibly about the fantastic state of religion in the U.S.A. He summed it up as crime waves but great interest in religion—juvenile delinquency, but the Sunday Schools are crowded—racism but much talk of Christ's love—air bases around the world but big missionary programs—world philanthropy, but money-mad materialism. It was beyond him, but nevertheless he had to confess he liked Americans, even though he never expected to understand them.

Then he told us that this was choir rehearsal evening at his church and invited us to attend. Vera said she would be able to go. It would be her first opportunity to visit a Protestant church, and she seemed rather eager for the experience. Lorena and I arranged to meet her there at eight o'clock.

The church was within easy walking distance of the hotel, on a side street, inconspicuously and unpretentiously tucked away in a neighborhood of friendly homes. To reach it we finally had to go through a graveled alleyway where children, together with a couple of dogs, played in the dusk. People sat in the back yards and a radio blared out Russian music through an open door.

When we met Vera in front of the white wooden church, I asked her which appealed more to her, the cathedral or this plain, typically "old-Protestant" structure. She said,

"I would first have to be convinced of the appeal of religion."

"Do you think anyone could convince you of that?"

"I don't think anyone could," she replied.

The minister came out to welcome us, taking note of Lorena's cameras and flash equipment through the top of his bifocals as we approached. He explained that the choir had been rehearsing for nearly an hour, not for our coming, but because they loved to sing. The choir consisted of more than eighty voices, but since the people were laborers and some worked on night shifts, there were only some fifty in attendance this evening.

He led us inside under pieces of scaffolding where repairs were being made and paused with justifiable pride to let us look at the interior from beneath the balcony. The auditorium was small, seating perhaps three hundred; very plain and simply furnished, a kind of country church that one would find everywhere in our Midwest. On the white plastered walls were Scripture texts proclaiming in Russian that "God so loved the world . . ." and "I am the Light of the World . . ." and "Behold the Lamb of God . . ."

There were, of course, no pictures and no icons. The floor was plain boards, the wooden pews looked homemade, and on the chancel was a sturdy pulpit with an open Bible. But one had the feeling that everything here was exceedingly precious. The flowers on the pulpit, the hymn boards, the upright piano in front of the chancel were all important and seemed to say that the little church was greatly loved.

The minister escorted us to the "choir loft" which was actually a series of raised planks against the left wall of the church. The members rose to their feet when we approached. The director, a young-appearing man, stood at a lectern, baton in hand. We were introduced to him and then to the choir. They greeted us as if we were their honored guests. The feeling of friendship was spontaneous and genuine. They wanted us to know we had done them a signal favor by coming. Most of them (there were perhaps a dozen teenagers in the group) had met only two Americans in all their lives, Protestant ministers traveling under the auspices of denominational boards.

Everyone shook hands with us and had an enthusiastic, often excited word of greeting. Some covered my hands with both of theirs and let me know by expressions and words what they thought of America. To them America was a great nation, our people a great people, our churches great churches. "America is our Christian neighbor," they said. "Our Christian faith knows no barriers. Our Christ knows no hatred, has no suspicions, makes no distinction between people who believe in Him no matter where they live."

Our interpreter was almost as thrilled as we at this royal welcome. She seemed to be saying, "Do you see how friendly Russians are? This is the Motherland. These are the people and the people are the state."

The choir sang its first number. A stirring hymn about the majesty of God. The blending of voices was magnificent and the spirit of the singing swept away all barriers and differences in language or ideas. It sounded like a Cossack chorus. Lorena, who had permission to take pictures, momentarily forgot about her cameras and stood listening. The numbers were startling and magnificent, but nothing we could have said or felt paid the event a better tribute than Vera's sudden, yet quietly controlled, question, "Do people sing so beautifully in American churches?"

She said no more than that, but as the hymns continued, each seemingly richer and more beautiful than the preceding, she sat lost in thought, often as visibly startled as we at the glory of the singing.

How, I wondered, could religion fail to inspire people where it had this kind of self-expression? What could hold it back? This was like a return to Pecherskaya chapel. Once more it was the soul of the Russian people assuring us that the God who is praised is the God who is loved. Just now you wanted to say to the millions of Russians who had left the churches, "Come back and listen. One hour here, strengthened by faith, is better than your continual attempt to prove or disprove God."

After an hour in which the hymnody of Russian Protestantism seemed to ignite the faith anew in all of us who believed, I realized that the back of the church was crowded with people. They were seated in the pews beneath the balcony and standing, often families together, in the aisles. They had come, not to see the American visitors, but to listen to the choir and to see the faces of those who stood enraptured beneath the moving baton.

You could close your eyes now and feel a spirit of worship. You could imagine yourself in any Protestant church anywhere in the world where people love to sing. You could make believe you were back in your own church at home, only then you wished you could convey to American Protestants something of the loneliness you feel because there is such a gulf in understanding between the people of two worlds.

Russia, I said to myself, is only some eighteen hours

away from America in terms of time, but we are a hundred years apart in terms of understanding. We are so close we can communciate in minutes and yet so far away we seem never to reach each other's thoughts. We are hopelessly apart, yet we need only extend our hands to the people and we are one. You cannot listen to Russian music, Christian music, without wishing you had the secret for creating better relations between the U.S.A. and the U.S.S.R. If we could only meet the masses, if we could only persuade them we have nothing to promote but friendship, nothing to bring but peace, nothing to sell and nothing to gain but the fellowship of understanding—what a great adventure it would be.

But even as I was thinking in terms of religious adventures, one was being plotted for me at this very moment. I say it was an adventure because I am no singer; certainly not when compared with these Russians who were making the church resound and who were luring in the neighbors.

It was natural, however, that at the conclusion of their rehearsal one of the younger members should come up with a request which Vera gayly interpreted. "Would the visitors from America sing a song for them?" My interpreter took it upon herself to intrude for the first time with an opinion of her own. She was sure that anyone with a name like Bach should be quite capable of filling such a request. Her opinion was endorsed by a chorus of voices, inferring that it was surely the Lord's wish that I should turn church soloist. They did not include Lorena in this because she was busily changing films. At such times she has a happy facility of being preoccupied with her cameras.

I tried to ease out of it without offense to the Lord or to Russia by saying that it was too bad no one had a violin because I would not mind playing a number, but even then I had a sinking feeling someone might rush out and hunt up a fiddle. I asked Vera to explain that years ago I used to play in church orchestras and knew all the songs from "Revive Us Again" to "A Mighty Fortress" but I urged her to emphasize that that was years ago. "Tell them," I said, "that though I memorized the melodies I did not know the words."

It was a lame excuse. I knew it was. Vera translated, "They say that they are not looking for musical perfection. They say they are not perfectionists either. They say they just want to hear a religious hymn, the kind sung in your home church."

I promised myself then and there that when I got back home I would begin learning the words to a dozen hymns right away. But that good intention did me no good here and now in the Baptist church of Kharkov. I was on the spot and I knew it.

But suddenly I came up with an idea. I say "suddenly" but actually it occurred to me only after I had taken an inventory of the songs for the entire liturgical year, realizing how many first lines I knew and how few first verses. I asked Vera to inquire whether they had "Silent Night" in their repertory, and they did. And I said it would be a wonderful idea for all of us to sing it together, they in Russian and I in English.

This was agreed to wholeheartedly, with the proviso that I first sing one verse solo, which I did. And the Russian people gathered that evening in the Baptist Church of Kharkov were the best audience—and the only one—I have ever had as a vocalist. And when I finished I was convinced of something else: "Silent Night" is effective no matter who sings it.

Then we sang it together. More correctly, I stood in the choir loft with them, while all around me people everywhere in Christendom seemed to be singing. After the song was finished a hush fell over the church, a silence so deep that the director laid his baton on the lectern with both hands so that it would make no sound.

A large, husky man at my side turned to me with tears in his eyes, took my hand and said, "*Slava Bogu.*" The choir members turned to one another without speaking. They merely glanced at each other for a moment or turned a hymnal over in their hands or put the book down on a chair silently or touched their hands to their eyes and then turned away. As I started back to the pew, they took my hand and one by one, they said, "*Mir, mir,*" which is "Peace, peace," and "*Do svidaniya*" which is, "A good farewell," or "*Spasibo*" which is more than just, "Thank you." But most of them said, "*Slava Bogu.*"

It was late when Lorena and I walked back to the hotel with our interpreter. The alley neighborhood was very quiet and the streets were quite deserted. A few women, attired in overalls, worked by lantern light, doing men's work in a ditch near the curb. Munching a piece of black bread, a very old man looked up at us and smiled. A group of workmen passed us. A street car rattled by.

As we crossed the street at an open corner, I saw the tower of the old cathedral on the hill against the moonlit sky. I wondered whether it might have heard the voices singing, "Silent Night," or was it much too lonely and too old to hear?

We hardly spoke all the way back to the hotel. There

was not a great deal to say. But when we parted at the hotel and an Intourist car came to take Vera home, Lorena said goodnight to her and I said, "*Slava Bogu*—is that better for a greeting or for saying good-by?"

"Either way," she said. "Tonight it is rather good—either way."

4. The Russian Trinity

In ROSTOV-ON-DON, in the land of the Cossacks, I sat one Sunday afternoon with an apostle of Jesus and a disciple of Lenin. The apostle was a gray-haired pastor of the Evangelical Baptist faith. The disciple was his granddaughter, a university graduate in the field of geophysics.

My interpreter was a solemn, composed young man, a party member, with a will to work. Throughout the morning he had carted me around from church to church in this lovely city on the Don River and now, in late afternoon, seemed as eager for another interview as I. He had an academic interest in religion but in all his thirty-three years he had never attended church.

The four of us sat together at a homemade table in an arbor in the back yard of the minister's home. The minister's wife had served us tea and Russian pastries. The flies were swarming and the day was hot, but at that there could not have been a better setting for our conference than this small yard behind the four-room parsonage. Here the minister often sat preparing his sermons and here the student frequently came with her books in geophysical research. Religion and science, so to say, had often held a rendezvous here, but never with an American listening in.

In Russia no one tries very hard to convince anyone about the value or need for spiritual faith. There is no evangelistic zeal, as we know it in the United States. No one sermonizes in public squares, preaches in tents or testifies on street corners. Such demonstrations are not actually forbidden, but they could be stopped by the law which prohibits teaching religion in groups of more than three. Ours was not a teaching session on this Sunday afternoon; it was a friendly get-together, arranged for me through the cooperation of Intourist.

The student sat across the table from me—a pretty, dark-haired girl of twenty-three with a pleasant and confident way. But for the lack of rouge and lipstick, she looked the part of almost any American coed. In Russia, education is a passion. It is also highly competitive. This girl was hand-picked for special study in a country which graduates twice as many scientists each year as we do in the United States. She was an out-and-out rationalist and an active member of the Young Communists League.

The minister, a resigned, humble man, sat at the head of the table, opposite my interpreter. Earlier I had visited his church, a very lowly place that had been adapted out of a residence damaged in the war more than ten years ago. The ambitious congregation of five hundred working people had equipped it with pulpit and pews and were building onto it now because attendance was growing. One of the members took me around proudly to show me the Scripture texts that adorned the walls. The texts were full of hope and promise: "The meek shall inherit the earth."

"One sheep and one shepherd." "The path of the just is as a shining light."

You could never imagine the minister preaching hell-fire and damnation, but you would have expected him to shake his head solemnly over the state of religion in Russia. For he impressed me as one who carried the weight of faith in the country dedicated to atheism. I had the feeling he probably spent his secret moments praying that God would produce some sort of miracle to help His cause. I expected him to speak his mind grimly and without excuse. He did not. He did exactly what other members of the clergy whom I had interviewed had done. He said with steady emphasis, "The Church and Communism can work together. There is no reason why they cannot."

I looked at him inquiringly. My glance must have shown him my surprise. It may even have betrayed the dilemma which was catching up with me more and more every time I interviewed a Russian clergyman or talked religion to a Russian believer. How wide was the gap between what these people told me and what they were really thinking? Did this suspicion of duplicity exist only in my mind, or was it actually a fact all down the ministerial and priestly line?

Not a single churchman would say a single word against the state. No one questioned any governmental action or criticized any governmental decree. I was constantly given the impression that separation of church and state had resulted in a new and happy era of cooperation between the two. Now this seasoned cleric was also assuring me that Christianity and Communism were compatible.

"Can Christ and Lenin ever be reconciled?" I asked.

His answer was quick and eager. "The love of God," he said, "reconciles all men."

"Is there no conflict between Christ and Lenin?" I asked.

His gaze hovered on me a moment. He listened and smiled patiently while the interpreter translated my question. He glanced at his granddaughter as if inquiring what she would say in answer to this.

Finally he said, "There is a conflict, of course, But there are many areas where Christ and Lenin can agree."

One minute I was sure he meant it. The next minute I was equally sure he did not mean it. This was part of the dilemma.

His eyes met mine. There was an impenetrable region I could not reach. It was not fair for me to judge him and yet, as he looked at me with a prolonged and guarded glance, I felt he was trying to advise me that there are times when one is forced to hide behind half-truths. There was a deep longing about him. There was a look that seemed to say, "I trust the interpreter and I trust my granddaughter, but I cannot get out of my mind the fear of being overheard. The days of suspicion are past here in Russia, and yet they have not passed."

I put the question to the student. "Can Christ and Lenin be reconciled?"

"Christ is a myth," she said confidently, as if she had got her evidence from some unimpeachable source.

"Are the Disciples also mythological?" I asked.

She looked at me as though this had never occurred to her. She looked at her grandfather as if for help. "I do not know," she said.

The minister chuckled good-naturedly. "Well, Grand-daughter," he said, "it is a good question."

She agreed and said she would give it thought.

"Do you ever go to church?" I inquired.

She shook her head negatively. "I feel no need for the church or for religion," she said.

At this point she gave the pretext of being coldly dogmatic and reminded me that party members are not permitted to belong to a church. She explained why this was so: Communism is based upon materialistic philosophy. The true Communist is always an atheist. Then there is also the matter of divided loyalties, the all-sufficiency of the Communist program, opposition to the superstitions which the church perpetuates and the intrigue which has always been part of the church's history. All of this was spoken confidently, as if she got it out of a book. I was sure she believed what she was saying. I was equally sure she had doubts about it. This, too, was part of the dilemma. There was a longing in her eyes and a questioning she could not hide.

"As you pursue your studies in the field of geophysics," I asked, "do you become more or less convinced that there is an Intelligence or Power behind the universe?"

"Neither more nor less convinced," she said with a toss of her head. "There is no need for any external cause or first cause. The material world has no beginning and no end. Matter and motion give us all the answers we need. The more we learn, the more we realize that what were once considered mysteries are really not so mysterious."

"But, Granddaughter," asked the minister, "where does matter get its elements and where does motion get its motion?"

90

"They are inherent in themselves," she said.

"Well, well," he sighed, "I do not want to mix with you when it comes to science." Then he said to me with a wistful smile, "But sometimes she does mix with me when it comes to religion. I tell her that faith as well as science has its miracles."

We went on to talk about Communism and the Church and about all that has happened to the Church and Christianity in Russia since the Soviets came into power. Here, separated by two generations, was Russia, old and new. Here was religion on the defensive, challenged by the fresh, frank spirit of youth: religion with more convictions than it dared proclaim, and youth with more answers than it could justify. Here was young Communism exposed to the quiet, reflective influence of Christianity and more sensitive to it than it dared admit.

Between the longing that existed in each—the religious patriarch and the young scientist—there suddenly loomed the gigantic, unseen but sharply felt power of the state, a state so strong, so compact, so absolute, that it stood as a watchman entrenched in every life. Again I felt its power channeled through the personal life and thought of its subjects. It dominated their minds. It held its people within the unrelenting web of its power. It would not let the minister voice his deepest convictions. It would not let the student dream her dreams. And as I sat there, listening to my interpreter unhesitatingly translating, repeating, explaining, he seemed like a mechanism created by the state. I felt that in a way I was being influenced and guided by the state. Everything that I had heard back in America about Russia's regimentation of the souls of men broke over me with stunning reality. I wanted to say, "Let's tell each other what we are really thinking! Let's come out from behind our duplicity!"

We could not. We did not. I suppose we dared not. For forty years the world's strongest dictatorship has molded the mind of Russia, old and new. For forty years it has held a strangling grip on the thought of its people. Through the most intensively trained, highly organized and perfectly systematized network of authority in all the world, it has woven every area of life into a pattern of solidarity. Nowhere was this more evident than in the history of what had happened to religion in Russia since 1917. And as that story now unfolded I wondered whether Communism is not even more powerful in its ability to control the masses than most of us have realized.

I was asked to remember that the pre-Revolutionary church was an instrument of the tsars and that it lived under the illusion that religion could never be destroyed. I was also reminded that it was a disunited church, a church of indifference and a church asleep. When it awoke in 1917 and found the Bolsheviks in power, it tried in one leap to become the church militant. Frantically it urged its members to oppose the Bolshevik "servants of Satan," warning them that "the Christian flock and the bloody Bolshevik horde must be considered enemies until the end of time." Priests and pastors, bishops and patriarchs spurred their people to fight and resist the Red revolutionists. They organized the "Warriors of Jesus," a counter-revolutionary force, and blessed their weapons. They prepared slogans about pitting "God against Lenin," and "Christ against anti-Christ."

They also began talking about a united Christian front. In 1917 Old Catholics, Old Believers, Anglicans and

Orthodox decided it was time to get together. The leaders never actually united, but they talked about it and consoled each other with the belief that the Russian church could never die because of the fervor of the Russian people. They said they were the most religious people in the world and soon they would rise up against the Reds. They prophesied that God would put a speedy end to Bolshevik power.

The Reds responded by looting the churches. Then a mighty patriarch named Tikhon decided it was high time to do something about this blasphemy. He vowed he would do something about it. He did. He excommunicated the government. He censored the Reds in the name of Almighty God and ordered them out of the Church's fellowship. Some compared him to Elijah calling down fire from heaven upon the priests of Baal. But Tikhon conjured up no such miracle. The only thing he did was to get himself arrested while the new rulers, more powerful than the tsars, plundered more churches, stripped the altars, and paraded the streets, stopping only long enough to burn Tikhon in effigy.

Soon all churches were nationalized and church property became the possession of the "people's party." Soon church doors began to close. As they slammed shut, one by one, authorized reports began to reach the people. The government explained that church treasures had been confiscated and churches "robbed" only in order to feed the starving and clothe the naked and help the sick among Russia's wartorn and suffering people. A crust of bread is better than a Cross, they said, especially when there was an excess of crosses. They declared they had taken nothing out of the churches which in any way "infringed upon the practices of the cult."

Some people, hearing that gold and silver and precious jewels had been seized to feed the common people, felt this was a form of religion in action. Young Communists felt this way. So did people who resented the riches of the clergy and the hoarded wealth of the Church with its monasteries and lavish parishes. Perhaps, they figured, the Soviets were more "religious" than the religionists. Certainly they were more realistic. Here, at last, was the fulfillment of Lenin's promise that "Communism is a united league of class-conscious, progressive fighters, pledged to the welfare and liberation of the working class and opposed to the inconsistencies of the Christians who profess charity but oppress the masses." Let all churches everywhere take notice, they said, that atheism is more spiritual than organized religion.

But just when many Russians felt that Communism had some semblance of mercy and that the looting of the churches and the closing of cathedrals might be justified, the Bolsheviks seized forty-five clergymen, found them guilty of crimes against the government, and put them to death. Priests and members of the laity who showed hostility were speedily jailed.

The old minister had lived through all of this and yet he was telling me that Communism and the Church can and should work together. Which had changed the more, I wondered, Church or state, that these should now be reconciled?

At the height of the Revolution, the Church had branded the Soviets as beasts and anti-Christ. When Tikhon's excommunication proved ineffective, when the people did not rally to the support of the Church, the Holy Church Council of Russian Orthodoxy tried a new approach. Toward the close of 1917 it petitioned the Soviet government, requesting that the state recognize Church legislation and that no law affecting the Church be passed without the Church's consent. It made other demands. It said: we must keep our religious feast days, and we request that these be public holidays as they were in the past. We want our priests protected from insult and abuse. We petition you to make it unlawful for people to leave the church before they have reached the "age of consent." Religious teaching in the schools must be Orthodox teaching. The Church's property should not be confiscated. The government must give the Church a subsidy.

In 1918 the Soviets replied. They said they had given the Holy Council's demands careful consideration and were prepared to tell the Church exactly where religion stood in the new regime. "No church and no religious society shall have the right to own property," they said, "and all existing property of churches and religious societies will become the property of the state. We will permit you to use your churches on the basis of special arrangement with the local or central state authorities. You will no longer be permitted to keep civil records. Marriages will henceforth be secularized. Education will be secularized. The religious oath will be abolished. Teaching of religion will not be allowed in state, public and private schools where secular subjects are taught. There shall be no religious instruction to youths under eighteen in groups of more than three. The Church is separated from the state. Every citizen may adhere to any religion or to no religion. No one is allowed to evade his civil duties on religious

95

grounds. There will be no subsidies from the government and no church will be allowed to accumulate property."

To the Communists, to the young Communist as represented by the student geophysicist, this action was not merely right and equitable, it was necessary and inevitable. A government had finally arisen with the courage to expose a religion that had hidden behind the cloak of sanctity, that had set itself up as inviolable and divine, while actually being the instrument of capitalism and the servant of the bourgeoisie. Never before in history had the mask been torn from Christianity. Never before had the individual conscience been "liberated" and the souls of men "set free."

I asked whether the individual actually was free under Communism? Is this not a major difference between Christianity and Marxism? Take the matter of contemplative knowledge, for example. The very idea of personal meditation is considered useless and a waste of time to the Marxist. Marx once said, "It is not the consciousness of men that determines their existence, but, on the contrary, their social existence determines their consciousness." Consciousness is social before it is individual, he argued.

Who placed a higher value on the dignity of the individual than Christ? Was Communism asking us to believe that collectivism put more sanctity upon man than did the Christian faith? My disciple of Lenin said that was exactly what the world was being asked to believe.

She had her authority. Lenin, who master-minded the Revolution, told his followers, "Say to the clergy: if you are sincere you must stand for a complete separation of the Church from the state, for a separation of the school from the Church, and insist that religion be regarded *entirely and unconditionally* as a private matter. If you do not accept these consistent demands of liberty, it means that you are still a slave to inquisitorial traditions. It means that you are still hankering after government posts and the revenues attached to them, it means that you do not believe in the spiritual force of your weapon, and that you still wish to take bribes from the government. If this is so, the class-conscious Russian workers will declare ruthless war on you."

The Church not only obeyed. It capitulated. It had already abandoned the people to despair. The propaganda said, "Don't go to church. The church can do nothing for you. There is no God." "It looks that way," said the peasant. "It looks as if there is no God."

It looked that way when, in 1923, the Holy Church Council met and went on record with a series of amazing statements:

"The present world is divided into two classes: capitalist-exploiters and proletarians upon whose toil and blood the capitalist world is building its welfare."

"In the whole world," said the Holy Council, "only the Soviet Government of Russia has ventured to struggle with this social evil."

"The Holy Council pronounces capitalism a deadly sin and to fight it a sacred duty of the Christian."

"We see in the Soviet power a world leader for brotherhood, equality and peace among nations."

The Council then went on to condemn the Patriarch Tikhon as a traitor to the Church. "There should be no place for counterrevolution in the Church," it said. "The Soviet Power is not a persecutor of the Church; it is the only one which attempts by state methods to realize the ideals of the kingdom of God. Every believing churchman must not only be an honest citizen, but he must with every measure work with the Soviet Power for the realization upon earth of the ideals of the kingdom of God."

Small wonder that the minister should tell me that Communism and the Church can work together! Even Tikhon finally came around to the Soviet side. He affixed his holy name to a confession which said, "All my anti-Soviet actions, with the exception of a few minor errors, are summed up in the statement of accusation of the Supreme Court. Recognizing as correct the decision of the Court to hold me responsible for anti-Soviet activity. . . . I repent of these my transgressions against the state . . . I am from now on no enemy of the Soviet power."

So Tikhon was released, and clergymen who had alternated between pulpit and prison promised to be good. Russian Orthodoxy, which at one time had accused the Reds of murdering a thousand priests and creating ten thousand martyrs, admitted they could have been wrong. So the churches began to reopen. Priests began to come out of hiding. Some said it was a victory for the Christian faith, and others said that a more devastating blow had never been dealt religion anywhere or at any time.

How did the gray-haired minister feel about it? What did he think of religion in the U.S.S.R.? Would he care to comment on the Soviet victory, if victory it was, over the Church? What was his reaction to the persecution of ministers and priests in post-Revolution years?

He had his answer. "We are free to preach and worship throughout our land. No ministers and priests were persecuted because of their faith. They were imprisoned and executed because of antigovernment action and then only after trial and due process of law."

The student emphatically agreed. And what was there for me to do but to bury my dilemma and let the matter stand? Minister, student and interpreter were all agreed, it seemed, that I was not to probe any deeper. They sat there looking at me and I at them, and when I laughingly said I feared I was a poor inquisitor, the student smiled and said, "Be glad for that. Religious inquisitors were not good people."

But we did manage to bring religious history somewhat up to date. It was agreed that between 1923 and 1929 religious organizations outside the Russian Orthodox group occasionally resisted Soviet decrees, but the government brought them into subjection, one by one, and accused religious groups in foreign countries of inciting local churches to rebel.

During the 1930's the government's attitude seemed to be, "If you are foolish enough to worship, go ahead." In 1941 Russian statisticians presented some interesting figures: nearly fifty per cent of the people still held some form of religious belief. In 1917 there had been 54,000 churches in Russia and in 1941 there were approximately 10,000. Of these some 4,000 were Russian Orthodox; the others included Adventists, Evangelicals, Baptists, Mennonites, Lutheran, Roman Catholic, Uniats, Moslem, Jewish groups and certain Armenian-Gregorian churches. Today, I was told, more than 20,000 churches were open and restored.

The minister wanted to know if we had many atheists in the United States. I told him I had met several. They never actually denied God. They just ignored Him. They did not belong to any "Godless Society" of the kind organized in Russia in 1926. They were usually individuals who were going through an intellectual conflict at a time when their old indoctrination was fighting it out with new scientific and philosophical ideas. These momentary atheists eventually found a faith somewhere among America's 250 denominational expressions or, if they did not, they never became very vocal about their anti-religious views. I explained that our atheists and agnostics in the United States were generally strongly individualistic. Usually they were more anti-church than anti-Christ.

"There is a religious consciousness in America and everywhere in the world for that matter," I said. Then I asked the student, "Is it possible that this consciousness exists here, too, and Communism is expressing it among Russian young people? In other words, do you find the security and joy in Communism which people generally find in religion?"

The minister said, "I will answer for her. She cannot answer because she has not entered into the religious experience."

"But, Grandfather," the girl warned, "how can you answer for me when you have not entered into *my* experience?"

"Well, well," said the old man, seemingly as proud of her wisdom as he was sorrowful about her faith.

The girl wanted to triumph. "I have found everything I need in Communism and in my work," she informed me quietly.

Addressing her with a term of endearment, the minister asked in great earnestness, "But have you found peace, true peace for your soul?"

Her words betrayed a touch of emotion as she replied, "Of course, I have found peace. Now let us proceed to find peace for all the world."

"Yes, yes," agreed the minister. "That is true. That is the greatest assignment."

Again I came back to the question: Is Communism a religion? And we discussed the matter for a long time with the disciple of Christ and the disciple of Lenin talking freely and dispassionately about their views.

The answer I found to the question on this Sunday afternoon in Rostov-on-Don was, "Yes, Communism is a religion." It is a systematic religion which, in its highest ideal, believes that the state is God, work is worship, and a better social order is the promised land. It has its trinity, consisting of Marx, Engels and Lenin. Undergirding all of the foibles and blunders and inconsistencies of which we may rightly accuse the Soviets, the philosophy of these three men remains the cohesive force which keeps Communism respected and intact. It is impossible to understand modern Russia without them.

They came into the conversation again and again: Karl Marx, the father of Communism; Friedrich Engels, the great collaborator; V. I. Lenin, the practical demonstrator.

Soon the battle lines were drawn, not only across the wooden table, but across all of Russia and, as far as the girl was concerned, through all the world. The pastor spoke tenderly of Christ's concept of the Fatherhood of God. The student parried it gently but positively with Marx's concept of the Brotherhood of Man and not in any vague and idyllic sense, but in what she considered the cold, hard facts of labor, production, wages, and the personalization of the worker.

Karl Marx, first person of the Communist trinity, was presented by the student as a realist who took nineteenth-century social, political and religious liberalism out of books and put it to work in people's lives.

Marx was a Prussian, ruthlessly brilliant and a revolutionary against tradition. The problem of religion played an important part in his early life. His parents followed the Jewish faith only superficially and became Protestants when Karl was six. They felt they needed a religion for religion's sake. Karl, at seventeen, thought differently. Religion, according to his views, could be put on and taken off as easily as a jacket and it was better to take it off. In fact, it was imperative to take it off and keep it off if you would be a good working materialist.

That is what he was, a materialist. His religion was philosophical materialism. He dissected it, analyzed it, reformulated it, preached it, and sometimes almost lived it.

"Remember," he once warned a friend, "I am really not a very good Marxist."

But he was an iconoclast and proud of it. Before he was twenty-four, three universities had felt the impact of his daring views, and one at least, the University of Jena in Thuringia, read his proclamation, "In one word—I hate all the gods."

These were the words of Prometheus, the Titan, who stole fire from heaven and gave it to man. For this, Zeus chained Prometheus to a mountain and commanded a vulture daily to gnaw at his liver until some god consented to die in Prometheus' stead.

I could have read all sorts of symbolism into this in the arbor behind the parsonage, for it occurred to me that perhaps Christianity would have to die in Communism's stead before the people realized what they had lost when they lost a vital, living faith. Marx, first person of the materialistic trinity, had stolen their fire. That is, he had taken away Christianity's appeal for the loyalties of a people. He had crossed the minds of youth with a challenging, formidable stride. He had commanded them to think even at the expense of their dreams, and work though it meant denying themselves and destroying the old institutions even before the new had been tried.

Yes, I could have read symbolism into Aeschylus' Prometheus, but Communism is no symbol. It is starkly real, fiercely contemporary, having in it ideas that all too often jibe with youth's deepest disillusionments and agree with youth's gravest discontent. Communism is tremendously vital in the life of someone like the student geophysicist who has intense ambition and who believes she has been called to build a better world. Communism is a religion with her and with other young Communists who have taken courses in the "History of Atheism," who have studied religion in the light of its relationship to class struggle, who have been shown the fallacies of faith and the negative influences of institutionalized Christianity, who have had it "proved" to them that materialism is founded on natural science and that Marxism is absolute truth.

Throughout most of his sixty-five years Marx was a dominant figure among political philosophers. He borrowed from Plato and plagiarized from John Locke and owed more to Hegel than he could ever repay. He took the absolute idealism of Hegel and applied it to his own absolute realism and whatever there is of the "spiritual" in Marxism was stolen fire from the German philosopher Hegel, who dominated the metaphysical views of the nineteenth century.

We talked about Marxism, the student and I, through

the unerring and consistent aid of my interpreter. He *was* a mechanism, a highly proficient working machine in the realm of languages. The minister had lapsed into a protective silence, content to listen. Apparently, he had been over this ground many times, had struggled with it in his mind and wrestled with it in his heart. He sat there as if pondering how he could ever deny what he believed or how, in the face of an overwhelming majority, which included the entire youth of Russia, he could formulate any convincing defense. Frequently he looked at me as if to ask how he could convey to me his feeling about the Russian trinity and the Trinity to which he had dedicated his life. To speak or to be silent. That was his problem. Sometimes he sighed and his manner said, "There is no way out. I must hold my peace, even though my silence denies what I know to be true."

So his granddaughter spoke. There were things she had to say even if it might mean hurting the old man. Marx *was* challenging to her and Christ *was* only a myth to her, and all of her training and indoctrination were along these lines. More than that, Marxist philosophy fit perfectly into her geophysical studies. It was Marx who first implied the eternal existence of matter. It was Marx who explained that the permanent basis of truth is objective reality.

Yet it was not Marx alone who created the philosophical structure of Communism. There was also the second person of the materialistic trinity, Philosopher Friedrich Engels, who said unequivocally, "Karl Marx is a genius. He stands higher, sees farther and takes a wider and quicker view than all the rest of us put together."

Engels was a rich man's son. His father was a manufacturer of cotton goods in Manchester, England. In 1870

Engels and Marx founded the First International in London, which was a union dedicated to improve the lot of the working people. Behind it was the unfolding philosophy of materialism. Behind it was Hegel and the formidable force of a Hegelian idea: the dialectic.

No one can appraise Communism without an understanding of the dialectic; no one can appreciate what Communism means or understand Russian religion or the lack of it without considering the impressive power of the dialectic process.

Hegel's dialectic method was a scientific approach to truth in the realm of ideas. This is what it meant: the first stage or statement of an idea is called the *thesis*. This *thesis* contains within itself its own contradiction or antithesis. The clash of thesis and antithesis, much like a brainstorming session, results in a synthesis which, combining both thesis and antithesis, is much nearer truth than the original thesis. This process of thesis challenged by antithesis to effect a synthesis was Hegel's general concept of the dialectic. He acknowledged that he got the system from Plato, and used it in the realm of idealism.

Marx and Engels applied the dialectic in the field of realism. They got it from Hegel and they put it to work in a way which gave history a new twist. They said that all life and nature can be explained best in the light of the dialectic. In fact, life and history proceed along a course set by the continual clash of thesis and antithesis, or as the process was called, "the doctrine of opposites."

Hegel said that *ideas* contained contradictory natures within themselves. Marx and Engels said that *matter* also contained its own contradictions. Hegel insisted that ideas were continually moving toward a higher truth through the dialectic. Marx and Engels said that the materialistic world is moving toward Absolute Truth by means of the same process, and they cited the struggle of class against class as their great example.

"A class of people," Engels insisted, "is determined by the economic development of a given period, by the means of production and by the theories of the time." Capitalism represents the thesis, the workers the antithesis, the new regime which evolves out of the clash is the synthesis. The synthesis itself again takes the form of a thesis. Soon it is again opposed by its antithesis and another synthesis evolves. *Truth*, according to Marx and Engels, is found in each synthesis, but it is only relative truth. Absolute truth is found in only an ultimate synthesis.

"The world," said Engels, "is not to be comprehended as a complex of ready-made things, but as a complex of processes."

In the compelling style of the materialistic gospel which he and Marx wrote, they declared, "Eternity in time, infinity in space, mean from the start and in the simple meaning of the words, that there is no end in any direction, neither forwards nor backwards. It is clear that the infinity which has an end but no beginning is neither more nor less infinite than that which has a beginning but no end. The material world is an infinite process, unrolling endlessly in time and in space."

It was this type of mind, Engels' type, fluent and creative, coupled with the intellectual wizardy of Marx, that challenged thinking people, glamorized the masses, and was today making a strong bid for the souls of Russian youth of the kind who sat with me in the parsonage arbor.

It dawned upon me that Communism might have conquered half the world had it not insisted upon setting itself up above God. This was a stumbling block which the masses would not tolerate in the nineteenth century and which they would oppose again today. This was the frightening element in Marxism and the silent specter in Communism. By denying God they made themselves superior to God. Marx and Engels would have none of Him, nor would they let the people rest who had found solace and power in religious faith. Nor did the third person of the materialistic trinity let these people rest. Lenin, demonstrator of the dialectic, most important political figure of modern Russia, schoolmaster's son, brilliant lawyer, powerful speaker, incessant writer, the man who trained the one-time theological student, Stalin, and without whom the "people" might never have revolted. Lenin, like Marx, hated the gods.

"Fear created the gods," he cried, "fear before the force of capitalism which is blind!"

"All contemporary religions and churches," he told his audiences, "all and every kind of religious organization, Marxism has always viewed as instruments of bourgeois reaction, serving as a defense of exploitation and for the doping of the working class. The struggle against religion cannot be limited to abstract ideological preaching. The party of the proletariat must be the spiritual leader in the struggle against all kinds of medievalism, including the official religion."

The churches had to go. God had to go. The materialistic trinity demanded *Lebensraum* for its idea. The years of Lenin, 1870 to 1924, were filled with a ministry of atheism unparalleled anywhere in the world. If any modern Christian had had half his zeal, all of Russia could have been Christianized. Imprisonments, exile, his life almost constantly threatened, his mind filled with fury against the exploiters of the "masses," continually accused of being a tool of Germany, he stormed the land with a slogan, "Peace to the huts and war to the palaces!"

"I do not preach war against God at all costs," Lenin said, "that only helps the priests and bourgeoisie. I am a materialist, that is, an enemy of religion. I am a dialectical materialist, that is, one who fights against religion not in the abstract, not by means of abstract, purely theoretical propaganda, equally suited to all times and places, but concretely, on the basis of the class struggle actually proceeding—a struggle which is educating the masses better than anything can do."

And when the Revolution broke, when Lenin incited the Bolshevik "liberators" to action, when the "ten days that shook the world" jarred the sleeping religionists into terrorized action, the Communist trinity blessed and sanctified the conquest.

It is possible to conquer a country through power, but it can be held only by a philosophical ideal. This ideology Marx forged in the fury of his passion against the bourgeoisie. Engels made it graphic and understandable. Lenin incorporated it into a party and branded it upon the consciousness of a nation. It became a faith, a doctrine, a religion beyond all religions, based not upon "images, visions and revelations," but upon the cold, hard facts of life and what men can do about them with the intelligence at their command and the power at their disposal.

The minister, the student, my interpreter and I talked until late afternoon, but I doubt that we were any nearer reconciling Christianity and Communism than when we started. I doubted whether they could ever be reconciled. There is a great gulf between a trinity of materialistic moderns who, in the words of Lenin, taught that "the idea of God keeps people in slavery," and the Man from Galilee who declared that fellowship with God sets men free. Did the interpreter think these could be reconciled? His single answer was the good, hard Russian, *"Nyet."*

But the cleavage between contemporary religions and Marxism is not always sharp and clear. There are areas in which they reluctantly meet and sometimes tacitly agree. I realized, even as I sat in the parsonage yard, that these areas built a bridge between the apostle of Jesus and the disciple of Lenin.

The "reconciliations" we talked about made sense to me, but I had the feeling if I ever put them into a book I would be in for no end of criticism from good churchmen who have painted Communism in the blackest black (or the reddest red) and who picture Marx, Engels, and Lenin as bearded men in baggy pants who never had a constructive thought in their heads and never set forth a single original idea.

Such critics were never more wrong. Dangerous as the Russian trinity may be, subversive as their plans may seem, deserving as they are of the titles, "God killers," "church haters," and "antichrists," we should by rights understand where Communism and religion tend to rub shoulders in our modern world. This is not to mollify the godless teaching of the materialistic trinity, condone the action of the Bolsheviks or respect the violent atheism of the Soviet. It is simply sitting for a moment at a listening post, so to speak, between an apostle of Christianity and a disciple of Lenin.

First of all, Communism has an ethic. It has ideals to live by and a code to live up to. I realized this again in my association with the young geophysicist and other young Communists I had met and interviewed recently in Rostov-on-Don. I realized it in my acquaintance with the interpreter. These young people have a high moral code based upon the Platonic idea of the good, the true, and the beautiful. Membership in the Young Communists League enjoins a special devotion to morality, a morality which often borders on Puritanism. Lenin insisted it was unnecessary to base morality upon God or, what he called, "anything outside of human society." He based morality and ethics on the "facts and needs" of life, particularly as related to the struggle of the proletariat. A person should be good, he insisted, simply because he lives in a world with other human beings.

Marxism believes there is a permanent basis of truth which can be arrived at over the long, hard route of the dialectic. This, in a way, is also not incompatible with Christian thought; at least, that part of it which believes we advance through struggle and we learn through experience. Perhaps what Marxists call the "leap in the dark" is not what we construe as faith or revelation, but there is a touch of kinship between the two. We Christians, too, have our objective ideals. They are formed in our mind through sense-perception, and the ideal thus formed lures us on. This, too, is to be found in the philosophical concept of Communism.

The Communist speaks of his "better world," his new "social order," his "workers' utopia." To the Communist youth this idealistic state is a kind of new kingdom which the world has never known or seen. He believes it may have to be built upon force. It may require another revolution to lead men into a "classless world."

The Christian, too, has his idea of a better world. He sees it evolving out of love and understanding. The minister expressed the Christian viewpoint when he said, "If we believe in God and if we believe we are all children of God, we have a working basis for the brotherhood of man."

"But," argued the student, "religion makes a distinction between those whom you call 'children of God.' In one country religion recognizes a system of castes, in another a system of creeds, in another a system of color lines, in still another a system of economic distinctions."

"If you will examine religion more closely," mused the pastor, "you will see that it is these very injustices and inequalities which religion seeks to overcome. You must distinguish also between true religion and false, just as you differentiate between true and false Communism."

In seeking for "similarities" between religion and Communism, an interesting point of agreement was found to be man's independent search for truth. To many outside the U.S.S.R., the Soviet "separation of church and state" may be nothing but subterfuge or domination of religion by the government or a trick to lead the church into total eclipse. Young Communists think differently. They believe it is the honest fulfillment of Lenin's plea that, "the state must not concern itself with religion, and religious societies must not be bound to the state. Everyone must be absolutely free to profess whatever religion he likes or to profess no religion. There must be no discrimination whatever in the rights of citizens on religious grounds."

111

The minister noted another area where Christianity and Communism might be reconciled. Marxism, though it denies God and does not see the universe as purposive, does, nonetheless, believe in an ordered world, a place where, according to Engels, "Nothing happens without a conscious purpose and an intended aim." But here the similarity seemed to end.

The minister insisted that the world had purpose and intelligence and that God had determined the nature of things in accordance with His law and plan.

The Communist student admitted no such "infinite design." Her answer to the question of life was "matter and motion." Everything in nature carried and perpetuated its own within itself.

The pastor said it is divine law that governs the world. The student said it is chance.

The clergyman contended that lasting knowledge comes through God, through a study of the Word and, perhaps, even through preaching.

The young Communist reminded us politely that Lenin had insisted that no books, no preaching, no religion can possibly enlighten anyone, unless he is first enlightened by "the struggle against the evil of capitalism."

My dilemma remained, despite our long discussion, despite the tea and pastries and the skill of our interpreter. I still had the feeling that the minister was restrained by an unseen force which we in democratic countries have never known and cannot understand. His mind was not fully his own and his opinions were those which forty years of Soviet rule had steadily imposed. I suppose we in the U.S.A. accept our religious freedom too lightly because it has been attained too easily. Here was a man who had to be careful not to oversell religion or undersell his Lord, and the result was almost incomprehensible spiritual inhibition.

Here, on the other hand, was a young Communist with an atheistic conviction, also beyond the grasp of the western mind. We in America have never been subjected to any teaching so complete and intensive, so designed to suppress and liquidate the natural quest of the individual for a relationship with Something higher and greater than himself. It was almost with longing for an affirmative answer that she asked me whether I thought a truth could be arrived at by any other than the dialectic method or that it could be proved by anything but science.

I said that a mystical demonstration which takes a hopeless, useless life—as religion often does—and transforms it into a hopeful, useful life, also proves a truth. I suggested that it is no more fantastic to think of uselessness being changed to purpose than it is for matter to be changed into energy.

She said, "It is not the same."

But her grandfather spoke up eagerly and asked, "Why is it not the same?"

"Because," she said confidently, "the discoveries of science can be seen even by the unbeliever, but the discoveries of faith must be seen by believers."

I suggested that she was not a believer, but I felt sure she would have to admit she recognized her grandfather's faith and what religion had done for him.

To this she replied, "My grandfather is a good man."

The minister shook his head and smiled.

At this point Lorena arrived in a taxi which the interpreter had ordered to bring her. She came into the parsonage yard loaded with cameras and decided the light was still good enough for several pictures. She had even brought my Polaroid and we all had a good time talking about the wonders of science and what a remarkable world we were living in, and there was no disagreement among us about that.

But after our good-bys, I felt a sense of loss and loneliness for both the minister and his talented granddaughter, especially for her because I wished she might have had the chance to talk with American students and American scientists and learned their views on the place of God in contemporary science. I could not help thinking it was something of a tragedy that she knew so little about the strength of Christianity and so much about its weaknesses. It was something of a tragedy, too, that we who profess the faith often fail to live and demonstrate it. She had no belief in the value of spiritual contemplation or the power of prayer, nor in the merit of one's relationship with a personal God. The idea of religion as worship had never actually occurred to her. And all of these were things which all of us Christians believe and all too few of us sincerely practice.

In a way I even felt a bit sorry for my interpreter, though I do not know why I should have. He was such a self-sufficient, capable person and he seemed to respect all people regardless of their views or their place in life or their faith or lack of it.

When we drove back to the hotel together, we were still talking about Jesus and Lenin and about the need for man believing something and worshiping something.

"Tell me frankly," I said. "Do you never feel the need for God or religion?"

His answer was, *"Nyet."* And *"Nyet"* in Russian always seemed a bit more final and more severe than just plain, "No."

5. *Lonely Are the Godless*

O<small>N A</small> S<small>UNDAY AFTERNOON</small> in Rostov-on-Don I went around to the Cathedral of St. Alexander Nevsky, which was open for worship, and bought an icon I had looked at several times before. There are vending counters in most Russian Orthodox churches where you can buy candles and sacred bread and, occasionally, an ancient icon. The price for this one was certainly right, about twenty dollars in American money, but the size and weight had made me hesitate. It was a bronze-framed head of Christ in a sixteen-by-sixteen-inch glass-enclosed shadow-box inlaid with strips of polished copper. The halo encircling the dark and brooding face sparkled with gems, above which was a miniature dove of peace, skilfully carved. The icon weighed about eight pounds, was evidently quite old and one of the finest I had seen for sale.

As I walked out of the church with it, a great crowd of worshipers followed me. Even several beggars hobbled to their feet, indicating they wanted to examine the icon and honor it. So I held it up and they made the sign of the cross and murmured prayers I did not understand. One old woman started to cry, and a crippled woman came forward and kissed the glass door that covered the Messianic face.

Religion, as far as these people were concerned, was still explosive with emotional appeal. Evidently their religious impulse had not been sublimated in the state. They were determined to honor the Christ and informed me by signs and phrases that my icon was the counterpart of worship. They believed there was holiness attached to it and power emanating from it and fortunate was I for having procured it for my very own.

A smartly dressed Russian woman, coming from the church, stopped to ask in English if she could be of any assistance. She remained for a moment, a striking contrast to the predominantly peasant worshipers. She explained that there was both veneration and superstition connected with icons and even a belief that some icons were not man-made at all, but had come down from heaven. These, of course, were especially effective in working miracles. Some of the people, I suggested, certainly acted as though mine might be one of them.

"I don't think so," she laughed. "These people are just naturally religious."

With this she walked away, leaving the icon the center of attraction.

These, of course, were old people, pre-Revolution religionists. I wondered what the icon would mean to the eighty million young fledglings of Mother Russia who know Christ only as a myth and have been taught systematically that religion is but an instrument of oppression.

I found out what it meant to one of them when I got to my hotel and laid my purchase momentarily on the manager's desk. A young Russian student spied it and came over for a closer look. I asked him what he thought of it. He shrugged, smiled patiently and said, "It's not an Andrew Rublev." This was certainly true. Rublev was the master icon maker of the fifteenth century and his works are priceless.

Then the young man wanted to know what I was going to do with it, since I was not Orthodox. When I explained that I collect all sorts of religious objects, he looked at me in bewilderment. Such articles have no function, he figured, and since they merely perpetuate superstition, they should be put into museums. The government has the right idea, he believed, in preserving religious art treasures to show the folly and extravagances of the early churchmen and to remind people of the unbounded greed of the tsars.

During our visit together, I put to him several questions which I had been asking wherever I had the chance: Does Communism satisfy an impulse to worship and a will to believe in Something or Someone higher and greater than oneself? Is Communism a valid substitute for religion?

His answer was typical. "Religion is false. Communism is true. Of course, Communism satisfies me. What more do I need? What more is there? We have it all."

Nonetheless, he was quite interested in my field of research. I again sensed a genuine curiosity about the religious life and about my ideas on religion. He began to query me on why I engaged in this kind of work and what the relationship between religion and American life actually is. Whether all this was mere curiosity or a secret longing was difficult to say. I rather suspect it was a genuine interest in the religious phenomenon as we know it in America, and a certain wonder about the startling fact that we Americans cannot conceive of a country without

*Women workers were constructing high, new walls and shaping
the chalk-white stones with expert skill.*

A Russian flower vendor in front of her stall.

The Metro is a super-subway, a series of underground "cathedrals" or stations, artistically constructed in granite and marble and without question the most remarkable in all the world.

The Kremlin, this ancient citadel of the tsars, contains three magnificent cathedrals, six churches, four palaces, and a number of museums.

Across Red Square the divine mother of all cathedrals, St. Basil's, stands decked out in full canonicals. Its multicolored onion-shaped dome, its haughty tower, its majestic and haunting grace have kept their vigil over the Kremlin fortress for three hundred years.

*They wish to pray in these holy spots, but prayer had gone out
of fashion.*

It was communion service. . . .

Also present were three scholarly young Russians, students for the Baptist ministry.

I have heard "God Be with You till We Meet Again" sung in many places, but never with more sincerity and spirit than here in the Moscow Baptist Church.

I felt the spirit of the millions who have persistently refused to let Communism destroy their will to believe.

God or devoid of what we call the spiritual ingredient.

He wanted to know if I really believe that a nation can not exist without God? I said that was one reason I had come to Russia. His response was typical. He gave a low murmur of incredulous, thoughtful wonder. *Why* couldn't a nation exist without God? How, he wanted to know, would I explain that nations *with* God often failed? Nations *with* God were guilty of more sins than Russia could ever be. Nations *with* God had appallingly bad records, he thought.

Once, he reminded me, when a Christian accused an atheist of invoking God's wrath to the extent that a great drought covered the land, the atheist said, "Why doesn't God permit rain to fall on your land, at least?" God or no God, he insisted, what happens to one person happens to all. The Pope dies just the same as anyone else, and the Patriarchs were just as eager to keep on living as was the lowliest peasant. And, he maintained, there is no difference between Russia and America, either, except, of course, that Russia is superior and more advanced.

He could not get over the fact that America is still so "saturated with religion." It was a great mystery to him. As great a mystery as Russia's religious void is to me. We did find several areas of agreement, agreement about the contrasts between our two countries.

We agreed that, whereas in America it is fashionable to belong to a church, in Russia it is more fashionable to stay away. In America it is honorable to love God and revere Christ; in Russia it is officially more honorable to deny God and ignore Christ. In America, religion is applied to life, integrated in life and considered an essential part of life. In Russia religion is shunned. We have made religion vocal and newsworthy. The Soviets have banned it from their radio and press. These things we agreed on.

As I sat with my icon on my lap, talking about religion to this friendly young Communist, I wondered how he would react if he were suddenly transported to America for a quick look at some of the fantastic expressions of American faith. Imagine him getting a glimpse of the flamboyant highway signs: JESUS IS COMING. ARE YOU READY? Or the all-too-familiar WHERE WILL YOU SPEND ETERNITY? What if he saw JESUS SAVES scribbled on rocks across the length and breadth of our countryside. Or noted LISTEN, SINNER, GOD IS WAITING despoiling an overhanging cliff. We take these things as a matter of course. We even put up crosses to mark the spots where people have met death on hills and curves. This young man had never seen the inside of a church.

What if I were to show him one of our Saturday night church pages? *The Los Angeles Times,* let us say. Or what if he were to hear the religious songs on our juke boxes, or the prayers that open and close many of our radio stations, or what if he viewed a spiritual healing service on TV or heard the radio recitation of "Hail Mary, full of grace," or if he were exposed to the religious beat included in a floor show or heard our politicians when they waxed evangelistic or joined in singing, "When the saints go marching in!"

Happily, before I was tempted to describe the enigma and wonder of our kaleidoscopic pattern of faith, a taxi came to take Lorena and me to the Rostov dock. We were booked for a three-day steamer trip up the Don and Volga rivers to Stalingrad.

I said good-by to the student. He offered to carry the

120

icon out to the cab, which, I thought, was a courteous act and quite a concession on his part. And, as was often the case, when we parted and I asked his name, the answer was, "It does not matter. We will probably not meet again. But it was nice to have met someone from America."

The elderly porter who helped us put our baggage into our six-foot-by-eight-foot cabin stood in absolute awe when I propped the icon on the little writing table. He was in his seventies, attired in a tight-fitting black suit, with a black cap pushed back over his white hair. Definitely a pre-Revolutionist Christian, he shook his head and purred in wonder at my "Rublev."

His wrinkled face took on an ecstatic expression when I indicated the icon was to stay on the table for the duration of the trip. He doffed his cap and started to make the sign of the cross. Looking at me as if asking whether I, too, was of the faith, he touched his forehead, his breast, his right shoulder and his left and bowed low. With signs and words, he inquired where I had got this possession and why. I managed to tell him and he nodded and murmured over the icon again. Certainly for him the symbols of faith had never died and the impulse to worship was still at his finger tips. Shaking his head and commenting on the icon, he started to leave. I tried to tip him, but he was offended. With exaggerated gestures, he seemed to say, "How could I accept any money in His presence!" So he hurried away thanking me for whatever I had done for him.

There was no question about the quality of these Russian peasants. They were sensitive, gentle, long-suffering, and kind. The hold of our modern, two-decker steamer was full of these *muzhiks*, as the peasants are called. Lorena and I passed through their quarters when we came aboard. A hundred or more men and women were patiently trying to make themselves comfortable on the floor, hemmed in by bundles and baskets amid coils of rope and boxes of freight. Here below, where they were riding, the heat was intense and the stench from the washrooms almost unbearable.

Our first-class cabin on the second deck was pure luxury compared with steerage where the peasants rode. Communist Russia is still a long way from a classless society. We had two comfortable bunks, a wash basin and a handy clothes closet. A small dining room for first class passengers —about eighty of us—was located astern, and up front was a lounge with chess tables, an upright piano and the ubiquitous heavy red plush draperies on large circular windows. Our traveling companions included Russians from various republics, most of them on a workman's holiday, a group of teenagers, and several well-dressed Russian families. The head of a textile factory in Kharkov had told us that in the Soviet Union everyone who works gets an annual vacation with full pay. The average vacation is two weeks, but people who do heavy work may get as much as five weeks. People who need medical attention can take their holidays at a health resort and arrange for free, special treatment. All summer resorts and sanatoria are operated by the government under the Ministry of Public Health.

The peasants down below, whom Lorena and I called the "icon-lovers," were not on vacation. They lived in settlements along the river and had been to Rostov-on-Don for trading purposes, riding steerage for a few rubles. The river steamer was a symbol of the contrast between old Russia and the new, between the icon-lovers down under and the iconoclasts on the upper deck. Here were two worlds: the long-suffering, pack-burdened travelers, and the carefree, strolling crowds who enjoyed, as we did, the beginning of our upstream conquest of the thousand-mile-long Don. Here, too, was a graphic lesson in Russian religion. Whereas the old tsarist regime had assured its icon-loving-subjects that religion and suffering were inseparable, iconoclastic Communism was telling its people that all talk about being patient under adversity has ever been a capitalistic plot. Happiness, said the party line, has nothing to do with holiness, and joy is by no means a by-product of faith.

While I occupied myself with thoughts of this kind and while Lorena roamed the deck taking pictures, a good destiny led me into the company of two passengers who spoke English. The young woman, Rya, good-looking and primly dressed, was a secretary in a Stalingrad governmental office. Joseph, a Ukrainian, was a foreman in a tractor plant.

We sat together in the comfortable lounge while the peaceful countryside with its meadows and cattle ranges, slowly unfolded on either side of the narrow Don. Children played on the sandy banks and occasionally we passed a quiet village whose whitewashed homes glistened in the afternoon sun. My newly found friends were actually eager to talk about religion when they learned my purpose in coming to Russia. They told me soberly they were "anti-Christ" and saw no reason why they should be anything else. They, too, contended that Communism was "spiritually" satisfying, that it had its moral and ethical standards, and that it adequately explained the meaning of life. They were happy and adjusted in their knowledge of it.

We decided that American religion in its modern emphasis had at least one element in common with Russian atheism. To most of us Americans, Christianity has come to mean a happy adjustment to life and is designed to help us acquire abundant living, peace of mind and soul. We in the western world no longer believe that the Lord chastens those He loves. We believe He blesses people. We even go so far as to suggest that God wants His children to be well to do. If the Soviets are in league with dialectic materialism in order to find happiness, we, in the western world, are in league with Christian materialism to reach a similar goal. While we talked along these lines, Joseph took pains to remind me that if American religion is justified because it makes people happy, then anything that makes people happy is justified, and anything so justified is undeniably religious.

But belief in God, as far as he was concerned, is either an indication of an inferiority complex or self-delusion or a plot of some kind. Christianity, he contended, is founded upon premises which are untrue or upon propositions which can not be logically proved. "Christians," in his opinion, "are people who think that by talking and preaching about morality they automatically become more moral than non-Christians."

Despite all this, he and Rya were interested in seeing my "Rublev." They were also somewhat fascinated by the dubious fact that I was ready to cart a religious "relic" through the U.S.S.R.

They accompanied me to our cabin, examined the icon critically and were quite impressed. Rya wanted to know what it cost. She said that when she was a child, her parents had an icon in their home. It was gone now. A casualty of the war.

"So you collect things like this?" Joseph said. "Does that make you more religious?"

"I never thought about it one way or the other," I confessed. "I do it as a hobby."

"And you keep adding and adding to your hobby? When do you have enough?"

I told him his question reminded me of what a Hutterite once asked me when he visited our home. I had proudly showed the Hutterite my collection of some two hundred rare colored cruets. After he had looked at them for a long while without voicing an opinion, I asked him what he thought of them. He replied, "They are very nice. But what do you want with so many?"

"Good for him!" exclaimed Rya. "That was a very good question."

Then she and Joseph asked who the Hutterites were. I explained that they are people in the United States and Canada who live communistically.

"Communistically?" they exclaimed in unison. "What do you mean?"

"Didn't you know," I said, amused, "that we have communal societies in the United States? Communistic experiments have been tried in our country for more than a hundred years, and they are still being tried."

Frankly suspicious, they asked for more information. I explained that throughout the history of America certain groups had given the communistic life a serious try. I informed them that mutualistic living according to a communal pattern had been attempted in our country 129 times. At least, I had a record of 129 such adventures in communism. These included the Amana Colonies, the Shakers, the Perfectionists, the Icarians and the many others who had insisted it is possible to create a classless society and live more happily collectivistically than under free enterprise.

My listeners sat entranced.

"Come, come," said Joseph. "Is this actually true?"

I assured him it was. These experiments were indeed communistic to the extent that all property was owned by the group. The members sought security more than freedom, were willing to be regimented, invested their energies and talents and time in the improvement not of self but of their society, believed wholeheartedly, or said they did, that cooperative living, which renounced private enterprise, constituted a more advanced economic and ethical system than any ever proposed or produced under "capitalism."

My Russian couple could not believe I was telling the truth. Would a country like America permit anyone to adventure in Communism? Preposterous! All they had ever heard was that America refused Communists permission even to visit the United States and that we accused every last one of them of subversion.

I do not know about that, I told them, but I do know that of the 129 attempts at communistic living, 128 have failed. One hundred and twenty-eight of them had given Communism an unhindered trial, some for fifty years, some for twenty, some for only a year or two. Then they gave way to private enterprise and embraced the "American way."

Only the Hutterites, who came to America from the Ukraine in 1874, still persist. They are hanging on doggedly and desperately, trying to prove that a classless society is possible. Was their experiment growing? Yes, from within. The Hutterites are the most prolific people in all the world. But I had to explain that even the redoubtable Hutterites, the last of the communistic experimenters in the western world, are now in transition and are beginning to be considerably more "capitalistic" than communistic in their outlook and practices.

I had never realized how significant these communal attempts were until I discussed them in the presence of my two Russian friends. It had never quite dawned on me that the minority experiment of the Hutterians actually represents a "little Russia" in its insistence that the commune life is more important than the fate of the individuals who compose it. It is a "little Russia" in its iron-clad discipline, its exclusiveness, and its authority, whereby the commune bosses allocate the work and set the wages and regulate the activities for their captive subjects. The Hutterites are like a huge collective farm. They are a miniature U.S.S.R., with the great exception that they are avowedly Christian. This, I had to tell my friends, is the major difference between the Hutterites and the Soviets. There is a saying, "Under God, Communism thrives among the Hutterites. Without God, it fails in Russia." The Hutterites claim they are living according to a Scriptural injunction which affirms that the early Christians had all things in common.

"That," exclaimed Joseph with a hearty laugh, "is a bourgeois justification if I ever heard one. Certainly it is a claim we have never made. We do not need the Bible to justify our system. It can be justified on the basis of progress and common sense."

At this point Lorena came in to change films in her Medalist and Leica. Her moods are usually measured by

127

her luck with the cameras and I knew from her attitude that things were going well. Wherever we went in the world, the first line she learned in the native language was, "Please, may I take your picture?" She tried it out in Russian on Rya and Joseph and they were delighted. So off we went to the deck.

The river was beautiful, the meadows on either side peaceful, almost idyllic, with an occasional glimpse of small, adobe-like homes and roving cattle of a collective farm. Tugs bearing lumber and grain and oil drifted past us downstream. The Russian passengers seemed as thrilled as we with the start of the trip. They stood watching their land unfold before them. Parents pointed out scenes to their children, young couples strolled the deck hand in hand, and the group of teenagers was in a real holiday mood. Their trip, I was told, was a reward for work well done at a Rostov school. As I mingled in the crowd and felt myself a part of it, I again realized that people are pretty much the same all over the world, ourselves included!

But this only deepened the Russian mystery. Atheistic materialism insisted, in effect, that one should never say to oneself, "Behind the world with all its beauty is the Great Designer." Instead, it told its subjects, "When you walk with nature it is foolish to think there is Someone within all of this with whom you can identify yourself. When you watch the clouds or behold a sunset, it is silly sentimentality to say, 'The heavens declare the glory of God and the firmament showeth His handiwork.' And when you are caused to suffer with nature, never meditate on the meaning or try to find anything redemptive in the experience. It is only a delusion to think that Someone is saying, 'Fear not, I am with thee.' "

It was difficult to remain objective when I contemplated religion and the Soviets. Was Communism interested in anything higher than that which can be attained through work and human planning? Was there ever any rising above sensory perception? Think of a nation robbing its people of the fellowship of God! Think of the audacity of men who reduce the love of Christ to fiction!

With these thoughts plaguing me, I went into the cabin and jotted down my reactions. Clipboard in hand, I made myself comfortable on the cot, gave the icon a glance, and impulsively put down the following impression:

> Communism is totally rationalistic, thinks only of this life, plans only in terms of physical needs. Birth to the Communist is a biological phenomenon, life an inexplicable mystery, man the product of his environment, and death the final, inevitable extinction. Life's only purpose, according to the Communist line, is to make men more "realistic" so that they may better adapt themselves to what must ever be an existence without spiritual hope and an aimless journey into nowhere.

While I was stubbornly convincing myself of these things and recording them, I was also asking myself whether all this was any reason for opposing Communism or fearing it or wanting it destroyed. By what right did I condemn the Russian if he wished to follow his trinity instead of mine? If he had a complete cynicism about objective truth, that was his business. I reminded myself that if it is really true that no nation can exist without God, then

Communism will ultimately destroy itself by reaping the atheistic whirlwind it has sown. I had always been taught that it is not enough to understand only the Evident and the Seen; it is necessary to arrive at some idea of the essence of things, the Unseen. "Where there is no vision. . . ."

My thoughts were cut short abruptly by a song. A thrillingly wonderful song full of joy. The group of teenagers was putting on a spontaneous concert, and Lorena swung open the door calling to me to come out. Thoughtfully, I re-read what I had written. "Communism is totally rationalistic. . . ."

The singing flooded the cabin. It reminded me of the stirring Russian Doukhobor songs which I had recorded in British Columbia. I thought about these people, fugitives from their homeland, fanatically religious according to our point of view, mad about God and "worldless" as the Hutterites. I thought about the choir rehearsal in Kharkov when the group of Baptist believers sang "Silent Night." I thought of the church-going peasants in the Cathedral of Saint Nikolai and at Pecherskaya and in other churches I had visited. I remembered the students who always had a searching light in their eyes when I talked about religion and asked them about their deepest beliefs. I wondered how anyone could determine the depth of spiritual feeling or measure the capacity for faith in any individual. What is religion? What should it do? How can you define it and by what standard can you appraise whether it is wholly true or wholly false? All this while the icon remained inscrutable, and the solemn, thoughtful face of the Messiah said nothing more than, "Judge not that ye be not judged."

130

I joined Lorena on the deck where the concert was in progress. Singing, as was proved in the Baptist Church in Kharkov, is certainly not my forte, and Lorena again took advantage of every excuse to hide behind her camera, but here the informality and my almost forgotten experience with a barber shop quartet finally paid off. At least, it proved conclusively that nothing is quite as universal as a good song and there is no better portfolio of good will than a repertory of folk tunes and spirituals. "Home on the Range" brought the Russians on board closer to the spirit of America than any diplomatic speech, and the "Volga Boat Song" took us nearer to the heart of the Russian people than any guided tour could possibly have done.

Incidentally, when the Porgy and Bess Company came to the Soviet Union several years ago, they did more to break up the "hate America" program than any other method had ever been able to do. People in Leningrad wept when the Porgy and Bess players left town, and at Christmas time Radio Russia broadcast carols sung by the company, the first time songs of the Christmastide had been heard on a Communist radio since the Revolution of 1917. "Russia loves a heart that sings," was Rya's translation of a passenger's comment, and I requested her to tell him that this sentiment was shared by Americans as well.

That evening we had a songfest in the lounge and the following night another. In the midst of a storm, while the boat twisted and tossed, we were again entertained by the singers and tried to entertain them in return. By then we had left the channel of the Don to enter what Russia claims is the largest man-made "sea" in the world, the Sea of Tzimlyanskoe, twenty miles wide and one hundred and ten miles long. It is reached through a series of huge locks, claimed by the Soviets to be the biggest and most magnificent that man has ever made.

Photographing the locks was strictly forbidden, but Lorena's fingers were itching to include them in her pictorial documentary. Making the approach to each and every lock were monuments sixty and eighty feet high. They were actually marble pillars surmounted by statuary. Most spectacular among them was the towering statue of Stalin, emerging prophet-like from the horizon at the entrance to the Volga.

My casualty in the storm was one broken icon. When I returned to our quarters I found my "Rublev" face down on the floor in the midst of broken glass. I picked up the splintered frame and the few jewels which had fallen out and was happy to discover that the brooding face and the dove of peace had not been desecrated. The incident seemed to me a sentimental symbol of religion in Russia, as if the storm might have been the hand of Marx flinging down the icon to the accompaniment of his notorious phrase, "I hate the gods!" I wiped the bits of glass from the face and set it back once more on the writing table. We had just now entered the Volga, the mother of Russian rivers.

I looked out at the barren eastern shore, the region of the vast steppes running down to the Caspian Sea, against which lumber barges were moving with their huge cargoes. The sun was brilliant. The water of the river was a powerful, eternal force. I thought of the Ganges and the Jordan and the Nile, holy rivers which Lorena had photographed. If Russia has a holy river it is Mother Volga. The passengers on our deck, even those to whom the trip was a commonplace, were reverently silent.

Mother Volga is a romantic river, steeped in legend and

132

history. A chapel marks the spot where it rises in the Valday Hills. Along its 2400-mile journey to the sea, it flows past the shadows of cathedral domes and monastery walls. Up this longest river in Europe came the invading Tartars, while the Russian defenders were borne down on its crest to oppose them. The Germans fought for control of the Volga in World War II and the destruction of a thousand vessels filled the waters with Russian dead. A legend, probably confused with Marco Polo's narratives, related that at certain points where convent grounds touch the Volga's edge, fish appear on the first day of Lent, remain until Easter Sunday and then disappear as miraculously as they came.

Faith is a river. Perhaps, I told myself, religion in Russia is like the Volga which cannot be held back or conquered or despoiled. But, like the Volga, spiritual faith, in Russia, is full of governmental locks, a secretly constructed dam or two, and a man-made sea.

The "locks" in Russia's river of faith are governmental restrictions, some official, some psychological. The "dams" are the unyielding control of church property by the state and the state's rigid hold on the growth of organized religion. It can regulate it at will. It can hold it at a desired level. It can utilize its power. The man-made "sea" in Russian religion is modern Russian Orthodoxy, wittingly or unwittingly the ready tool of the state.

Russian Orthodoxy today represents a religious nationalism fully as thorough as it was in the days of the tsars. The Church is free only within the limit of the law which governs it. A governmental council works with the Orthodox denomination and a similar council works with non-

Orthodox bodies and this, too, is part of the man-made "sea."

The river of faith is Communist-controlled. There is freedom of worship in Russia only as far as freedom is granted. There are no church organizations as we know them in America. No young peoples' groups, laymens' movements, missionary activities, evangelistic crusades or Sunday Schools are allowed. No minister or priest preaches a social gospel unless it follows the party line. No public function ever includes prayer. No religious leader dares criticize the government. No Communist Party member may join a church.

Still the Volga flowed. And the symbolism I read into it made me wonder if religion could possibly be held back. Who could read the soul of the Russian people? Who could say whether or not God was being worshiped in the private lives of those I had met? Were the masses biding their time, believing and praying that atheistic materialism would inevitably defeat itself? Was Russia, once the world's most fervently religious nation, still spiritual at heart?

Shortly before we reached Stalingrad, I had another partial, isolated answer to these questions. Joseph, the factory foreman, returned to my cabin. He came under the pretense of saying good-by, but he tarried for a long time at the door. For a time we talked about the storm. Did I know that Tzimlyanskoe Sea was formed by the largest earthen dam in the world, nearly ten miles long with a height of over a hundred feet? Was I aware of the fact that the joining of the Don and Volga had created a continuous water connection of 50,000 kilometers and that it had tremendous irrigational and hydroelectrical as well as transportational functions? The canal, I was told, consisted of thirteen locks, and what an engineering feat it was became evident only when I remembered that the Don is forty meters higher than the Volga. The concept of such a canal went back to the days of Peter the Great, Joseph informed me, but it remained for the Communists to achieve it as the result of skill and the five year plan 1951 to 1955. It now linked the Black, Caspian, Baltic and White Seas and had great naval and military significance—which, he explained, was the reason that pictures of the locks were prohibited.

But actually it was not the canal he wanted to talk about. It was, I soon realized, the Volga, by which I mean the flowing stream of faith. It was religion that he got around to eventually and the icon served as his excuse. When he noticed it was broken, he walked over to it, asking me what had happened. Then he offered to lend a hand at straightening and replacing the strips of copper inlay which had become disengaged from the frame. Eagerly and quite expertly he set to work.

Bending over the icon so that I could not see his face, he inquired, "Tell me, are Americans truly very religious?"

I told him I thought so.

Without looking up, he asked, "What do you mean when you say they are religious? Are they different from us? Are they better than we are? Are they happier? What does religion do for them?"

I explained that Americans believe that trust in God gives stability, security and order to our individual and national lives. Separately and collectively we are convinced that God figures in our destiny. My personal feeling is that religion gives dignity to life and that our freedom is encompassed within our concept of God.

He wanted to know how we acquired this freedom, how it works, and whether I honestly believe that God exists. What proof did I or anyone have of God's existence and what did I think about some ultimate purpose within the universe and what were my views on life after death?

There was little doubt about it; he was on as much of a spiritual quest as were the rest of us. The difference was, of course, that he found himself in a country where open inquiry about religion was unpopular. But his atheistic indoctrination had not blacked out the will to believe or, at least, the wish to do so.

A pretense of not really caring too much, a make-believe effort to repair the icon with difficulty when the task was actually quite easy, a casual remark—all of these could not hide the universal truth that man is by nature spiritual and something deep down within him is going to give God an upward look. Nothing will get in the way of that, Joseph's attitude seemed to indicate, not even space satellites. I felt just then that if this man is typical of most Russians, the Gordian knot of atheistic bondage is some day going to be cut in this incredible laboratory of unbelief, the Soviet Union.

The similarity between Joseph and any man, in any country, who keeps his religious questing under cover, was remarkable. He was again convincing me that wherever man lives, man worships or thinks about worship, and the centuries during which men's minds have wrestled with the divine mystery have not stopped with any stated time, nor been abandoned at the borders of any particular place.

Religion is part of the developing experience of every individual, Joseph included.

All of this persuaded me to say to him, "You asked whether Americans are different from Russians who are not religious. Let me ask you whether you are convinced that Russians are *not* religious?"

He looked out of the window to where the Volga flowed and finally said, "What do you think?"

"I think Russians, like any other people, are religious by nature."

"You may be right," he said. "You may be right and there may be no other way about it. A person can never get away from at least thinking and wondering about it." He feigned a laugh. "We cannot even get away from this fellow," he said.

"Who?"

He indicated the icon. "This One."

He leaned back, looked at it a moment, clamped his hands down on the writing desk, and got up.

"That's the best I can do with it," he said. "When you get to America it can be repaired."

He propped the icon up in its place, said he was glad we had been together on the trip, and walked out abruptly.

In a moment the ship's whistle blew sharply. I looked out at the dock and beyond the dock to a terraced embankment with seemingly acres of wide, white marble steps. Massive colonnades, white and clean, surmounted by symbols of winged victory, rose towering and strong against the open sky.

Lorena rushed in excitedly in search of her wide angle lens. She had been told that pictures of this dazzling approach to Stalingrad were allowed. Did I know that what

137

were now marbled terraces and huge Corinthian columns had once been the site of a solid skyline of business places? Had anyone told me that one hundred thousand air raids had been launched against this city? Did I realize that here the pick of Hitler's armies had been pledged to drive the Russians into the Volga and that it was here that Stalin called upon the people of the church to pray? And had I heard the saying that he who comes to Stalingrad without faith will find it here?

The porter came in for our bags. The ship was at the dock. I tucked my treasured "Rublev" under my arm and went outside with a feeling strangely akin to coming home.

6. Victory Without Prayer

W HENEVER I WALKED the wide, new streets of Stalingrad, the miracle of the city's rebirth could not be hidden. Destroyed down to the last building, reduced to powdered brick and tangled steel by the full force of Hitler's might, Stalingrad is today once more a leading industrial center with a will to live.

Its population of over half a million is predominantly employed in tractor and steel plants, canning factories, oil refineries and shipyards. Northward is the great new Volga River dam, three miles wide, carrying a superhighway and a railroad right-of-way across its top. This is the most gigantic hydroelectric project in the eastern world.

Only the parks of rest and culture and the broad, open esplanade along the Volga betray the tragic past. Everyone knows that thousands of dead lie buried here. As in Kharkov and Kiev and a hundred other cities, war's victims were buried en masse. In the first German air raid against the city, 175,000 citizens of Stalingrad were wiped out. Altogether Russia lost 7,500,000 soldiers in the defense of the motherland, 2,500,000 more persons died of hunger, and millions more were maimed. The bloodiest of battles was Stalingrad. The turning point of the war was here in this city.

Hitler called it a walled fortress and a Red Verdun. He once issued the premature report that Stalingrad had fallen. The Soviets responded with a pledge, "There is no land beyond the Volga. There is no road of retreat. No sacrifice is now too dear for us, and deathless courage is our only cause."

I went out early one morning to find a Catholic Church where, I had been told, Mass was being observed. The full force of a people's determination to outlive the past was apparent at this sunrise hour. All around me workers were going forth to meet the destiny of another day. Against the walls of newly constructed buildings, two- and three-story-high-posters reminded them of the glory of the Soviet system and urged them to build bigger and greater than ever before, to raise more crops, better cattle, larger dairy herds. Radio loud-speakers recounted statistics on growth and achievement.

Who could escape the hypnotic pressure of this promotional technique? It goes on everywhere in Russia practically day and night. Caught in it, I could not help but feel the burden as well as the spirit of these people. Any American looking into the store windows would conclude that these people, in Stalingrad particularly, have nothing to live for but work, nothing to look forward to but hope, nothing to expect of life but the unending command to build. Store windows displayed the kind of clothing and wares that we associate with our five-and-ten-cent counters and our dollar stores. Shoes, clothing, appliances are scarce, expensive and annoyingly impractical from our point of view. And always the incessant march of the workers and the chant of the loud-speakers tell you that life is regimented, life is hard.

But as I walked in search of the chapel, I realized again that we in America have no cities where the parks are cemeteries and where life was once bombed down to the barest dust. We have been spared. To us much *has* been given, of us much is expected, and part of what is expected is tolerance and understanding and compassion. Many Russians have the feeling, and rightly, that their problems are more difficult than ours, their lives harder to live, their circumstances vastly different from those we know.

I paused to inquire about directions from a building custodian, who knew fragments of English. He took time to walk with me five long, open blocks. In appreciation, I gave him an English Missal which an American friend had given me. He was thrilled with it, patted it affectionately and said, "I would like it, but it is too much. Anyway, I am not Catholic."

"Keep it," I said with a laugh. "Neither am I."

"I am a non-believer," he replied. Then added, "Well, almost a non-believer."

"Almost a non-believer," I told him, "is almost a believer."

He laughed at this and decided to keep the Missal as his first gift from an American.

Lorena's reminder that "he who comes to Stalingrad without faith will find it here," came back to me as I joined the worshipers. There were not more than thirty, but the spirit of devotion was real and there was also a certain sense of freedom, more than I had found in many other churches along the way of our research.

Finding faith in Stalingrad is not too difficult. The historic battle line is memorialized with monuments of cannon. The bombed-out house and the gutted mill where the "victory or death" order was issued are shrines. Here the miracle offensive was born. Up on a lonely hill, a single tank marks the spot where the battle of liberation began and where the pick of the Nazi forces were sealed off, crushed and killed inside the Soviet ring.

My guide, a girl from Intourist, intimated that once it would have been impossible to walk here without stepping on the dead. Ever since the war's end Russian laborers have been clearing away the shells and shrapnel and shattered war material from these battlefields. But all one needs to do is scrape the ground to find layer upon layer of additional fragments, to say nothing of pieces of human bone.

Lorena took many pictures here, particularly of the women workers who were constructing high, new walls and shaping the chalk-white stones with expert skill. Our guide said that right where we stood the spirit of the "new Russia" had been born.

Another interpreter with whom I talked about the siege of Stalingrad had his own idea about it. He called it "victory without prayer." He attributed the triumph to faith, but he meant faith that had stopped counting the cost or the dead. He meant faith in tommy guns and sniper rifles, in hand grenades and mortars, faith in a Zhukov, a Rokossovsky, a Yeremenko and a Stalin. He called it faith in time, time which held back the Hitler terror for five months and four days, through one of Russia's fiercest winters, against one of Russia's bitterest foes. But he did not mind if someone—I, for instance—for sentimental reasons, wanted to believe it might also have been faith in God.

That was one man's point of view. There were many who agreed with him. But in Stalingrad I also found another man, a teacher, with a different idea. He had his own explanation of the victory at Stalingrad. He said, *"The dead were praying."*

I first met this elderly teacher by chance in the memorial museum where maps, miniature war models and dioramas tell the graphic story of the 149 days that "saved the world." Here, in these surroundings, he explained what he meant by the "praying dead." According to his estimate, these were men who once reflected the soul of Russia, a soul greater than that of church or state, a soul immortalized in the quest for God. He was thinking of Russian "saints," though not in the ecclesiastical or orthodox sense. He meant men like Dostoievsky, Tolstoy, Berdyaev. These were the dead who were praying for Russia's salvation. These were the ones whose spirits returned to help and inspire the people who saved the city. He felt that the power of these immortal dead had reached out in a mystical way to turn the tide of battle and that today they were making a strong bid to lead the Russian masses back to God.

The teacher was neither a churchman nor a spiritualist. He was simply one who felt that Communism's greatest mistake was its rejection of God; its greatest sin, denial of the immortality of the human soul; its greatest folly, an attempt to thwart the religious impulse. But for these mortal errors Russia could have gone on from the victory at Stalingrad to conquer the world without a struggle. So he believed.

This man was one of my most interesting discoveries. Did he represent a widespread, unvoiced opinion? Were there many like him, I wondered, who held these views? For here was a Russian who, in the very heart of the atheistic experiment, was willing to testify that the universe not only had meaning and intelligence, that life was not only purposive, but according to him, death was an extension of life and the departed were active in the affairs of the living.

He was of the opinion that many Communists secretly believed these things but were afraid to admit them. Afraid of what? Of other Communists. Afraid of the status quo. Communism is very strange, he said. The words and power of Lenin are still very subtle and very real. There is fear of Lenin even today though the man died shortly after the Revolution. This, too, is part of the "mysticism" in Russian life.

No one, the teacher insisted, lives apart from the past and this must be understood in order to understand Russia. No one is unrelated to the unseen and the spiritual world, be it good or evil. Every man is potentially a captive of the unseen powers to which he commits himself. Every Russian reflects the nature of his commitment and the source of his strength.

When he suggested that some day a "spiritual prophet" might arise in the land, a man who would effect a powerful influence upon the nation, I asked whether this could actually happen under the Communist regime. Would not any "prophet" or "saint" immediately be put down? Wouldn't his fate be Siberia or death?

"Our leaders may appear ruthless and bold," he ventured, "but they are not insensible to world opinion."

I could not agree. I reminded him of Poland and Hungary. He felt there were conditions and problems in these countries which no one but Communist officials fully understood. He believed there was more freedom and more tolerance and more intelligent leadership in Russia now than he had seen in his fifty-odd years.

I wondered whether even he, fearless and extraordinary though he might be, was instinctively cautious not to offend his Russian masters. He always came back to "the people." He felt it was the lack of a united voice among the people that caused the government to follow courses which might be contrary to the people's will. He contended that more churches would be open today if the people demanded them. More priests would be trained if the people insisted upon it. He always returned to his thesis that Russia lacks heroic men among the masses.

"The truly great of Russia are the living dead. And the living dead are praying," he repeated. "Some day their prayers will be heard and answered as they were answered at the victory of Stalingrad."

I met the teacher a number of times. I never learned what he was a teacher of, nor did it matter. In a world where science is king, who boasts about philosophy? Here was a lowly subject who had his examples of the power of the "praying dead" and was eager to share them with me.

He assumed that everyone in America had surely heard of Fiodor Dostoievsky, had read such books as *The Brothers Karamazov*, *Crime and Punishment*, *The Idiot*, and *The Possessed*. Surely everyone agreed that Dostoievsky was one of the world's greatest interpreters of man's search for God.

Communists had not rejected Dostoievsky, the teacher

explained. Naturally they had no sympathy for his sub-servience to the Romanovs. And they did not like what he said about revolutionaries. But they knew that his contribution to philosophy and literature was immortal. Talk to a Communist about Shakespeare or Voltaire and the answer would be, "We have Dostoievsky." They would even match him with a St. Paul or a St. Francis, knowing full well that a greater spiritual figure than Dostoievsky would be hard to find.

Dostoievsky, he wanted me to understand, was neither monarchist nor revolutionist. He was a symbol of the Russian spirit groping its way to freedom. That was why this writer was being referred to more and more in Russia. He was a growing power and a guide in the slow but forward-moving search for faith. Dostoievsky's prayers were beginning to reach out to the people in spite of the Communist web or perhaps because of it.

Did I know that Dostoievsky had been a friend of the Romanovs only because he hoped to influence the rulers to allow the peasants more liberty? Did I realize that Dostoievsky's friendship with the mid-nineteenth century revolutionists was for the same reason? Dostoievsky had the people at heart. He was searching for freedom for himself and for others. That was why he joined Petrashev-sky's political party. That was why he was arrested and condemned to death.

Had I ever read how, at the appointed time for the execution, three days before Christmas in 1849, Dostoievsky was led to the black-draped scaffold in St. Petersburg's Semenov Square? Did I know that at the very last moment, when he was being tied to the stake, when the firing squad had already filed in, an order came from Nicholas I calling for his reprieve? It was a plot. It was the tsars' way of torturing their victim. People who talk about the cruelty of the Communists have forgotten about the cruelty of the tsars.

Dostoievsky's reprieve was worse than death. On Christmas Eve he was led in chains past his home, so close that he could see the candles on the family tree, but he was not allowed to stop. Instead he was carried off to Siberia to begin a sentence of four years of hard labor, four years in which the ten-pound weights were never removed from his legs, even though he was a sick man, an epileptic, often at the point of death.

Then followed five more years of exile. But every Russian knew that Dostoievsky discovered God in suffering and Christ in pain, and that was something modern Russia was beginning to understand. For Fiodor Dostoievsky had once been an atheist just as the modern Russian masses were now assumed to be.

And Dostoievsky had his struggle with the unpredictable Unknown and he had his unanswered questions about the mercy and love which simple souls ascribe to God, just as Russians have their questions about these things today. The unwarranted suffering which often befell innocent people shook Dostoievsky's faith. He could not reconcile human suffering and divine compassion. His own afflictions were beyond reconciliation. Every time an epileptic paroxysm struck him, he died a thousand deaths. For days, during the aftermath, he was unable to remember where or who he was. Once when an attack seized him, he said, "I lay in the street like a whipped dog."

He also suffered from poverty and hunger and was continually haunted by the terror of his "execution" and

147

imprisonment. "He is like Russia," the teacher declared. "That is why he is so important for us today. We see ourselves in him. The nation's life today is like his life. We, too, have chains around our legs. But they cannot hold us. I am not talking about revolt or bloodshed. I am talking about the spirit. The liberation of the spirit. That is what Dostoievsky is talking about. The powerful character he created in Mitya Karamazov is himself. Mitya is Dostoievsky and Dostoievsky is Russia."

Like Mitya, Dostoievsky finally rose from the "purgatory of doubt by the grace of God whom he had condemned." On his way to prison a woman had thrust a Bible into his hands. At first it was only another burden, another weight to be added to those which his accusers had fastened on his arms and legs. But in prison he began to read and search its pages and whenever he did, he returned to the Book of Job to live through the calamities and furies of the man of Uz, the incredible symbol of patience who, in his moments of torment, said, "Shall we receive good at the hand of God, and shall we not receive evil?" At the turning of every page, Dostoievsky saw the story of his own life. In chapter after chapter he found himself. The book became the angel that guided him out of his prison of doubt.

He let Mitya say it for him, "The thought of God is tormenting me. That's the thing that's worrying me. What if He doesn't exist? What if He is an idea made up by man? Then man is the chief of the earth, of the universe. Magnificent! Only how is he going to be good without God? That's the question. I always come back to that. For, whom is man going to love then? To whom will he be thankful? To whom will he sing the hymn?"

The "longing for God" was the great thing. Goodness

to Dostoievsky was more than moral or ethical goodness. It was a capacity for the search for God and the courage to follow it. Today, according to the teacher, Dostoievsky's influence upon the U.S.S.R. is becoming incalculable. Nothing can hold it back. Few can escape its inspiration and appeal. Neither Communism nor atheism can withstand the mystical power of the "living dead."

"Dostoievsky is returning Russia to God as surely as God returned to him in the prison camp!"

It was an interesting speculation, this thought of the dead bringing a victory of arms to Stalingrad and now a victory of the spirit to the Russian nation. Did not we in America have our mystical guardians, too? Didn't we like to think that the spirit of a Washington, a Lincoln, a Jefferson, a Franklin, a Whitman watched over our country and influenced our destiny? Who was I to say these men were not calling us back to old ideals or leading us forward to new activities of mind and will? Who was I to question that Dostoievsky would be unable or unwilling to divinize the Russia of tomorrow?

It was Dostoievsky who said, "Nations are built up and moved by the power of the persistent search for God." It was Dostoievsky who contended that, "socialism is not merely the labor question, it is before all things the atheistic question, the question of the tower of Babel built without God, not to mount to heaven from earth, but to set heaven down on earth." It was Dostoievsky who cried out in tears, "What should I be underground without God? If they drive God from the earth, we shall shelter Him underground. One cannot exist in prison without God; it's even more impossible than out of prison. And we men underground will sing from the bowels of the earth a glorious hymn to God, with Whom is joy. Hail to God and His joy! I love Him!"

When Dostoievsky died, the Metropolitan of St. Petersburg came to pay his respects at the Nevsky monastery where the body lay. The celebrated cleric expected to find an empty church, but he found it crowded to the doors with praying students. People wept in the monastery yards, student groups intoned the Psalms and read passages from the Book of Job. The Metropolitan gazed on the scene and said, "They tell me these young men are atheists and that they hate the Church. What magic power has this dead man to bring them back to God?"

The teacher called it the power of faith and prayer. Dostoievsky, he said, left an unfinished work in Russia. When he lay dying he said he regretted most leaving the world before he had fully expressed himself. This unfinished task, the teacher declared, would now be completed from the realm of the "living dead."

Dostoievsky was praying.

He was not alone in this mission. Tolstoy was also standing in the shadows keeping watch over Russia and exerting his influence on the people. This immensely imaginative author-dramatist was, according to the teacher, becoming ever more important among the people.

I was inclined to agree. I had heard Tolstoy discussed frequently in Russia. Usually he was dismissed as "a good writer and a poor philosopher," but he was never ignored. The persuasive power of his idealism was once more catching the interest of the masses.

So was his sense of humor. A Russian who once asked me about the fanatical speed of American life, said we evidently had never heard of Tolstoy's "mathematical law."

This law said in effect that "the faster a man drives, the less necessary is the business to which he is driving. The rapidity of travel is in inverse proportion to its utility!"

Most of all, Tolstoy was being rediscovered because of his views on war and peace. He had believed implicitly in nonresistance and had sought to practice it. He used to say that the greatest part of the Bible is the New Testament. The greatest part of the Gospels, the words of Christ; the greatest words of Christ, the Sermon on the Mount; the greatest part of the Sermon on the Mount, the five commandments, and the greatest of the five commandments, "Ye have heard it said of old, 'Thou shalt not kill and whosoever shall kill shall be in danger of the judgment,' but I say unto you, that every one who is angry with his brother shall be in danger of the judgment."

"Tolstoy is coming back," said the teacher. "Everyone today is talking about peace and a new approach to the problem of war."

He contended that Russians were beginning to reassess Tolstoy's views on religion. After all, Leo Tolstoy had been a loyal member of the Orthodox Church for nearly fifty years before he began to ask seriously the inevitable questions, "What is the meaning of life? Where does it lead? Why are we here?"

"The questions Tolstoy asked are the questions modern Russia is asking," explained my informant. "You cannot drive them out of a person's heart by force. You cannot satisfy them by advances in science or promises of newer and greater mechanical achievements. There is a spiritual search that will change Communism if the search is sufficiently sincere. It will change it not by a revolution, but by the people's declaration of what they want out of life.

151

We will find the answers to Tolstoy's questions where Tolstoy found them, in the simple faith of the peasants."

My informant felt that the way of life and the hope of salvation which Tolstoy found among the peasants are things that neither Communism nor the Russian Church understands. It is impossible for the Church to understand them because organized religion and government are out of touch with what Tolstoy called the "inner light."

Tolstoy, he insisted, was praying, not for Church or state, but for the people.

When I told him I had spent considerable time among the Canadian Doukhobors who are ardent Tolstoyans, he was thrilled. The Doukhobors, Russians who left the Orthodox Church long before the Revolution, claimed that God was being replaced by secularism and accused both Russian Orthodoxy and tsarism of being partners in the crime.

The story is told of a Doukhobor who informed a Russian general that his people would never bear arms in any cause. Said the general, "How dare you refuse, when both Church and state tell you you must?"

"Church and state may tell us we must," replied the Doukhobor, "but Christ and Tolstoy have told us we must not."

After much discussion the general said, "I agree with you, it would be well to turn the other cheek if every person did the same, but as long as there are Turks ready to invade us, we must be ready to fight. The time for non-resistance has not yet come."

To this the Doukhobor replied, "Well, General, I don't know whether the time has come for you, but it has come for us."

There was an important point here, the teacher believed, not so much in the field of non-resistance as in the over-all struggle of the masses against religion and the government. Many modern Russians secretly believe that the "true faith" can never be found in an institution no matter how religious its name, or in a political party no matter how strong its power or its claims. More and more people are quietly working out their spiritual philosophy in their own hearts. The very authority which urges them to think realistically is at the same time unwittingly giving them the liberty to make an honest appraisal of their religious and political masters.

Tolstoy, said my informant, was speaking for modern Russia when he said, "For years I did not go to church. I no longer believed what had been taught me, but I believed in something. I believed in God, or rather, I never denied God, though often I could not have said what sort of a God. . . . But since I exist, there must be some cause for my existence, a cause of causes. That first cause is what men call God. As soon as I acknowledged that there is this force in whose power I am, I felt that I could live again."

The teacher looked upon the forces of organized religion with quiet contempt and upon Communism with a sigh of patient waiting. His strength and comfort lay in the knowledge that *the dead are praying* and as far as he was concerned nothing could stop the power of their prayers. It would be next to impossible for any Russian force or any American force or any other kind of force to keep God from His place in the hearts of the people.

Often when talking with him, I felt that his faith was a great deal stronger than mine; surer, certainly, in his concept of the "communion of saints." He meant, actually, communication with the dead and the influence of the dead in the lives of the living. It was more than a "guardian-angel" idea; it was unquestioned belief in the availability of a psychic force.

What an episode this really was! Here in Russia, a thousand miles inside the so-called Godless land, in the chosen city of the dead, discredited Stalin, I was learning about the nature of the Christian life. Even the most orthodox of our theologians would have agreed that here was the hint, at least, that life *is* a participation between the hosts of heaven and the people of earth. It came mighty close to our vaunted concept of the "mystical body" whose members, many believe, share one common life, have our spiritual well-being at heart and who, so we are often told, "aid us in our struggle against the flesh, the world and the devil."

My friend also included Nicholas Berdyaev in his saintly pantheon, insisting that when the religious revival begins in Russia, this eminent philosopher will have a voice in it. Berdyaev was the one-time Marxist in whom Christian idealism won a victory, a prototype of what could happen to the Russian intelligentsia who had never been reconciled to the existing spiritual void in Soviet thought. Tolstoy's appeal was to the masses; Berdyaev's, especially to the intellectuals.

Berdyaev opposed Communism on the grounds that it enslaved the spirit. He had no quarrel with its economic theories, actually, and saw a great deal of good in its collectivistic program. He was a socialist at heart. He might have remained a champion of Marxism had it not been for Marx's transference of personal conscience to

154

the collective state. This, he felt, led to a new form of idolatry, similar to the idolatry found in any form of nationalism. "God," said Berdyaev, "has laid upon man the duty of being free, of safeguarding freedom of spirit, no matter how difficult that may be, or how much sacrifice and suffering it may require."

Spiritual freedom was the keynote of Berdyaev's thought. He felt that Communism improved everything, yet improved nothing because it denied the soul's right to the quest for truth. Communism refused to accommodate people in their spiritual quest. It allowed no man's mind to live and move freely in the realm of search and discovery. Communism's theory was brotherhood, but its practical result was enslavement. Stripped of all glamour and high-sounding phrases, Communistic philosophy had as its goal the superiority of an economic process over spiritual principles.

"Economics must exist for man," Berdyaev argued, "not man for economics."

He criticized Communism because of its lust for material power and condemned western Christianity by the same token. He argued that it was just as disastrous for a free nation to live under the delusion that wealth is a sign of virtue as it was for a dictatorship to assume that the social forms of work are, in themselves, the supreme and only good.

Berdyaev believed that work is worship and true freedom is the "organization of society by such a means as will guarantee the opportunity of work and creation to every man." Whenever Christianity or Communism hinders or thwarts this ideal, each is guilty of dishonesty and aggression.

"Every man," said Berdyaev, "is made in the image of God, however indistinct that image may become, and every man is called to eternal life. The problem of class war is above all a spiritual and moral problem which involves a new attitude of Christians towards man and society, and a religious renewal of all mankind."

The teacher saw Russia as a battleground for these ideals as Stalingrad had been a battleground for proving a people's faith. He saw both Christianity and Communism confronted by the struggle of a people against enslavement. Tomorrow's religion in Russia, he predicted, would represent a vital, fresh and honest approach to faith and God.

There was a time, he made clear, when it was impossible to think of religious faith apart from institutionalized religion. There were rites to be performed and symbols to be understood and sacraments to be kept. Men felt that God and the Church were indivisible and that if they ever denied the Church they would be the victims of some terrible divine visitation.

Today, as far as he was concerned, that theory was no longer tenable. War, suffering, Communism have thrown the theory of an omniscient, infallible Church into the discard. God is a different God than He was when faced with the eyes of fear. According to Berdyaev and others among the "praying saints," man can determine his own fate in the present world and in the world to come. When he learns how far-reaching, how comprehensive and how explicit this fate can be, he will return to God with a deeper consecration than he ever knew under the Church's rule.

I was assured that when this "return to faith" actually took hold of the Russian masses, we Americans would be shamed by their devotion and embarrassed by their demonstration of religious fervor. "God always has purpose," the teacher warned, "and His purpose in Russia is to bring a new and higher form of life out of the spiritual chaos through which Russia has passed."

Such was one man's opinion. The "living dead" were praying and those who thought the victory of Stalingrad had been accomplished without prayer would one day learn the truth. Heaven, I was being informed, is on the side of the Russian people; and heaven meant not only God and Christ, but those also who had lived and died on Russian soil.

Priests whom I interviewed in Stalingrad smiled patiently at such a theory. Their attitude was the same as that of priests and ministers elsewhere in this largest country in the world. They had no prediction about religion's future except to insist that there is now, and will continue to be, a separation of church and state, and an ever-increasing freedom to worship.

One day I sat with three clergymen of the Orthodox faith in a cathedral at Stalingrad. The edifice, like most open churches, had been rebuilt from the ground up. One of the priests said, "Self-sacrifice restored the churches just as the sacrifices of self saved the city." He drew up chairs around a small table in the transept. At this ten o'clock morning hour a few women were grouped together in prayer. Making the sign of the cross over and over and bowing low in front of the icons, they also divided their attention between me and my host, the Archbishop Dneprovsky.

I learned from the archbishop that the Church's hierarchy consists of the Patriarch, who is elected by the nearly 100 bishops, presbyters and rank-and-file clergymen. The

Holy Synod is made up of six members, three permanent and three serving for six months.

I was told that the state does not interfere in ecclesiastical elections or in the affairs of the local congregations. The archbishop said he could confirm this out of his own experience. The separation of Church and state is definitely a reality, he reported. The Church now has seven seminaries and two academies located at Leningrad, Moscow, Kiev, Shitomir, Odessa, Stavropol, and Saratov. They are preparing some 2000 men for the priesthood. When I mentioned the Church's claim of 50 million constituents and said it seemed fantastically high to me, he assured me he considered the figure quite correct.

He said there were some 22,000 Orthodox congregations. The patriarchate of Moscow maintains jurisdiction over Russian Orthodox parishes in Teheran, Jerusalem, East Germany, England, France, and several in North and South America.

He told me frankly that the five restored churches in Stalingrad were deemed sufficient for the city's present needs. When more churches are needed, more will be provided, he was sure, by the people's government. I asked him how many worshipers came to the cathedral for Sunday services. He said about 1500. How many dropped in for daily meditation? About 150. What per cent of the communicants are young people of school and college age? He was prompt to say that ten to fifteen per cent would be found in this age category.

In answer to my question, "What is the main task of the Church?" his answer was immediate, "It prepares people for the next life."

"Do you think Communists who do not believe in another life and who do not avail themselves of such preparation will live again?"

He looked at me patiently and smiled.

"Are we to know or to judge either man or God?" he asked, as if to say that harmony with the government is more urgent just now than the defense of faith.

He claimed 25,000 communicants for the cathedral. He was proud of a new Bible published by permission of both the Patriarch and the government. It was a reprint of the Nikonian version first published in the third quarter of the seventeenth century. It used modern Russian characters while preserving the Old Church Slavic language.

I brought Lorena to the church later to take a picture of this new Bible but we could not get the required permission. However, the Archbishop and one of his immediate subordinates generously posed for us and treated us with a graciousness we will not soon forget. About these men was the same unspeakable sadness I had found in priests elsewhere in Russia. It revealed their inner depths more than words ever could. It gave a hint of their frustration, bordering on a kind of warning, as if in the quiet of their hearts they were whispering, "Do not ask me the cause. Do not ask me to explain. Just believe me when I say we trust and wait on God."

At such times the groups who hovered credulously around the icons seemed to me a good deal happier in their religion than did the priests. There was apparently no struggle in their hearts so far as conflict with the state was concerned. They had what they wanted, the right to worship as fully and freely as they wished. No longer were Red watchers lurking outside cathedral doors. No longer was worship disdained as in the years following the Revolution, or scorned and spied upon as in the days of the tyrant Stalin. Things were steadily getting better for the Church and, to the lowly worshipers, it was a growing sign that God is good.

This was often my feeling. There is another large group of worshipers in Russia, some 18 million who are known as the Old Believers. They represent the most formidable schism in Russian Orthodoxy and are today as doggedly sure of their position as they were three hundred years ago when they broke away from the mother church. At that time a peasant-priest rose to the position of a notorious ecclesiastical crusader. He was Patriarch Nikon who, like every other Christian reformer, argued for a form of faith based on apostolic "truth," the kind Christ would honor when He returned to earth again. Nikon set about to revise and "purify" the Church by correcting errors which, he claimed, had crept into the ritual ever since the faith was brought to Russia from Byzantium.

In the light of Russian religion today, or the lack of it, Nikon's proposed reforms can hardly be taken seriously. To the Communist they are absurd, another disgusting episode in the tragicomedy of faith. For Nikon demanded that the sign of the cross be made with three fingers instead of two. He insisted upon a threefold rather than a twofold alleluia in the liturgy. It was high time, he said, that these grievous errors be corrected and that the divine offense be removed.

God was troubled, Nikon told the people, greatly troubled at these liturgical inaccuracies. Equally troubled was Jesus because for years the Church had been misspelling the Savior's name. It was using *"Isus"* in place of *"Iisus,"* had been doing so for generations, and now the

160

time had come to make amends. Another thing, for hundreds of years church processions had been marching as the sun marches around the heavens when, actually, it was God's wish that His people march countersunwise! These were some of the Patriarch's issues at a time when the serfs were being bound to the land by intrigue and plot, corruption was running wild, and Polish and Russian Christians were slaughtering each other on the battlefield.

Backed for a time by the powerful influence of Tsar Alexis, who referred to Nikon as the "most intimate friend of my body and soul," the patriarch used his church reform as a plot for grabbing personal and ecclesiastical power. While the tsar was directing the military campaign against the Poles, Nikon managed the affairs of state like a dictator, playing both roles—the roles of pope and emperor.

Eventually Alexis broke with him, and the Church broke with him as well; but both state and Church, for reasons of their own, endorsed his proposed "reforms." Those who refused to accept them, who still insisted on making the sign of the cross with two fingers instead of three and of writing "Isus" instead of "Iisus," were now dubbed Raskolniki or schismatics and came to be known as the Old Believers.

Incidentally, the course of the sun, say the Old Believers, indicates precisely the course that church processions must take. Even today most of them consider it a mortal sin to go "countersunwise," or to pronounce the name of Jesus in three syllables instead of two. To eat potatoes is also still a heresy with many of them, for to them potatoes are the forbidden fruit of paradise. Tobacco is even more abominable. When Peter the Great asked them if smoking was worse than drinking, the Raskolniki said, "Smoking is worse, for the Bible says, 'not that which goeth into a man, but that which cometh out, defileth him.'"

But even the Old Believers, the ceremonial sticklers, broke up into two camps, so that soon there were the priestly and the priestless; and both were severely persecuted by church and state until the advent of Catherine I, who shielded all sorts of sects and was friendly to all sorts of schismatics.

Today, the leaders of the Old Believers still fight the battle for "Isus," and the leaders of Orthodoxy fight the battle for "Iisus"; and each in its own camp struggles for power, while their people make the sign of the cross with two fingers or with three fingers, and while the dead are praying.

A young Stalingrad Communist had this to say about it all, "Religion is perpetuated not by love, but by hate. Its history is the story of one group opposing another group. Neither Christianity nor any other religion could survive on the principles they proclaim. They grow only on dissension. They survive only on hate."

I discovered, however, that religion for individuals survived rather mightily on love, too; especially on love of God. It is dangerous to be prophetic, but the city on the Volga often tempted me to believe the maxim which said, "He who comes to Stalingrad without faith will find it here."

I had an interpreter, a girl of twenty-five, who refused to take any pay for the help she had given me in a number of interviews. When Lorena and I walked home with her, she invited us in for a cup of tea. The second-floor room she lived in was barren, cold. A few scant bits of furniture, a couple of unframed pictures, two improvised shelves of books and a sleeping cot were the furnishings of her "apartment." She made no excuses for its appearance other than to say, "Now you can see how a working girl must live."

In the cubicle which served as kitchen, Lorena helped her make up some cheese and caviar sandwiches. Tea was prepared on the rusted two-burner hot plate. But when we were served, the girl brought in a lovely silver sugar bowl. Because of our interest in antiques and because of the striking contrast between this valuable possession and the austere surroundings, we commented on it.

"Ah, that," she said. "That is all there is left of my parental home."

She then told us how, during one of the innumerable raids, she and her parents had crawled to safety underneath the basement steps. Did we know that this is one of the best places to hide when the bombs are falling? Of course, there is actually no place one can hide, especially if the planes carry phosphorous bombs. Their fire, she explained, shuddering, crawls everywhere like snakes, setting everything ablaze, especially the asphalt streets and even the ground. There is no escape at such times.

She went on to say that on this particular night when they crouched beneath the cellar steps it was "straight bombing." Her family had been miraculously spared then, but before the war was over she had lost both her father and her mother as well as her four brothers.

In forty-five minutes of strafing, the section of town in which they live was leveled. In the morning when they crept out through the rubble and debris, everything was gone. She remembered how open the sky seemed to her that morning. The shock of the night of terror was bad enough, but the most fearful thing to her was the unobscured view of the sky. Nothing hid it any longer. No roof tops, no buildings, no chimneys, no steeples pointed upward as a link between man and God.

She hoped we would forgive her sentimentality, especially since she could not adequately explain to us just what she meant or what she felt about the sight of the unobstructed heavens. It was as if she stood naked before the eyes of God, as if she had never realized until then how small and guilty one can feel when looking up into the vast expanse of blue and clouds. Even now, whenever she got out of the city, whenever she walked through open space, she relived that morning when she and God stood face to face where once had been her home.

Days later, while prowling in the ruins, she found the silver sugar bowl. Who could say how this was spared or why, or how or what protected it so that it suffered hardly a dent or scratch. It was a symbol and a sign. Of what? She hardly knew. She never went to church. She had rarely been inside a church. Never until the day she went with me had she spoken to ministers or priests.

She wondered if I could answer her questions. Since my field was religion, could I tell her why some people were taken in the war and others left? Why were some, like her father and mother who had never knowingly injured anyone, compelled to suffer more than others? Would I tell her, if I knew, why religion had so few answers for the great things in life, great things like peace and war, love and hate? Why, so often, did there seem to be no difference between religious people and the non-religious? Could I explain why innocent Germans died

164

because of Hitler, why innocent Russians died because of Stalin, and why even the wisest men know so little about God? How did I think American Christians would react if God were to take away their livelihood, their possessions, their loved ones and their joy?

Beneath her earnest questioning I, too, stood beneath the open sky. Just now I scarcely had an answer to the mystery of the silver sugar bowl, much less to questions about God and the Soviets.

There was an answer, but it required faith. Faith of a kind that had lived in a Dostoievsky, a Tolstoy, a Berdyaev, and of the kind that had not died in Stalingrad. I suppose the answer was: There is no victory without prayer, whether in saving a city or in saving a soul. They never lose God who have Him in their hearts.

To be sure, this might not be the whole answer and surely it was no easy assignment, always, to believe it. But in the quiet afterthought, amid the apparent hopelessness of these surroundings, I felt myself coming around to the teacher's point of view. It must be that the dead are praying and that, somehow, their prayers are ours as well.

7. *Wait for the Morning*

"MOSCOW THE HOLY!" That is how Napoleon described the city in Tolstoy's *War and Peace*. Madame de Staël, who figured in the French Revolution, viewed *Moskva* from the Kremlin heights and exclaimed, "Behold, another Rome!"

Visitors to Russia today have an appraisal no less sincere, "The showcase city of the Soviets!"

Their reference, however, is not to churches, temples or monasteries. They mean a modern metropolis which, compared to Russia at large, is like an industrial fair in a wilderness. Scrupulously clean, as most Russian cities are, Moscow's streets are doubly scrubbed. Its automobiles are ordered by law to be clean. Its parks of "rest and culture" are reflectively quiet. Its public squares are spacious. Its skyline is constantly growing, its buildings are dignified, its people, serious and proud.

Muscovites told me that their 34-story university building is the finest in the world, the G.U.M. department store the largest in the world, and the Kremlin the most spectacular governmental headquarters in this or any other world.

They may be right about the Kremlin, for this ancient citadel of the tsars, in a country now dedicated to atheism, contains three magnificent cathedrals, six churches, four palaces, and a number of museums, hoarding ecclesiastical treasures as priceless as those of its foremost rival, the Vatican. Jeweled crosses, gem-studded Bibles, silver chalices, gold icons, crowns, armlets, vestments and royal carriages occupy room after room.

I was assured that this entire hoard of holy effects now belongs to the proletariat. Nothing but cages of shining glass separate the sightseers from the heirlooms of their old oppressors, church and state. Only the alert and omnipresent guards keep the people from climbing into the great White Throne of Ivan the Terrible, or fingering the cross which once dangled at the breast of Metropolitan Nikhon. The clouds of glory have been rolled back. Here, as elsewhere in the Soviet Union, the masses roam the rooms of tsars and patriarchs. Even the domineering Tower of Ivan the Great, whose nearly 300-foot-high cross spreads its shadow over the red Kremlin walls, holds little terror for the common man. He has been told he is the conqueror and as he wanders through the sovereign grounds, it all seems true.

Outside the walls stands a hallowed shrine, a royal reliquary containing the ghost-like hands and heads of Stalin and Lenin. Rumor has it that heads and hands are all that remain, that the bodies have been dismembered, but the thousands who form the block-long queues show no concern. They wait with infinite patience in the rows of "worshipers" who move, a step at a time, through a burial garden where other Communists are interred. Gradually they reach the granite sarcophagus and finally pause in the mystic stillness of the holy tomb. Here they stand in a moment of supplication to whatever it is they believe in, a ceremonial of thought into which not even the sharp, intensive eyes of the guards can intrude.

Across Red Square the divine mother of all cathedrals, St. Basil's, stands decked out in full canonicals. Its multicolored, onion-shaped domes, its haughty tower, its majesty and haunting grace have kept their vigil over the Kremlin fortress for three hundred years. Like the cathedrals inside the Kremlin, it is now a "museum," no doubt the most notorious and magnificent one in all of Christendom. Built by Ivan the Terrible, St. Basil's has ever been an object for romance and superstition. Among the most popular legends is the much-repeated story of Ivan's ordering the architect's eyes gouged out so that he might never again create a building of such immortal beauty.

Lorena, of course, photographed St. Basil's and every other cathedral from every conceivable angle. She was convinced that the crowds who visited and revisited these once-hallowed places of worship did so because of a longing for something now lost. They wished to pray in these holy spots, but prayer has gone out of fashion. They are ambitious to recall the past, she thought. They have the will to worship, but not the privilege, while we in America have the privilege and, all too often, not the will.

It was easy to read almost any point of view into the mystifying medley that went in and out of the cathedrals. I remembered how an Orthodox priest told me that the ground on which a church is erected is forever holy and the spot on which the altar stands is like the footstool of God. Not even a patriarch can unconsecrate it. Though the church vanish and the altar be destroyed, the time will come, he said, when God will punish those who have defamed His house. Every Russian knows this, he assured me, as does every Communist.

And I wondered about this as the crowd milled in and out of the gilded and jeweled and icon-crowded sanctuaries with their frescoed walls. You could imagine any one of them to be Adullam's Cave or just a side show where the thin faces of Russian monks and martyrs leer down from every shadowy cupola.

Lorena was sentimental. She persuaded a policeman to take our pictures in front of St. Basil's. He wanted to know what we planned to do with it. When our interpreter informed him we would use it as a Christmas card, he shook his head in sheer unbelief and walked away. I wonder what he would have said of the finished product, for we did use it later, together with a picture of a chapel back home, and captioned it, "In Hometown Church or Kremlin Square, it's Christmas, Christmas everywhere."

If St. Basil's stirs the Russian masses with some sort of assurance that their leaders have triumphed over the past, there is an attraction underground which convinces them that Communism is also well equipped to cope with the problems of the present, even as their space satellites assure them to trust their leaders for the conquest of tomorrow. Underground, beneath the parks and palaces, beneath the ancient buildings and modern city traffic, is the Metro, which can be insulted if you refer to it as only "the subway."

The Metro is a super-subway, a series of underground "cathedrals" or stations, artistically constructed in granite and marble and without question the most remarkable underground railway in all the world. There are forty-five of these amazing stations, no two alike, with entrances so attractive that they are referred to as the portals of transportation.

To the 3,500,000 passengers who daily pass through this subterranean fairyland, Soviet achievement is real and spectacular, and it is no less real and spectacular to those who daily watch the Sputnik skies. We, too, made our easy pilgrimage down the long, steep escalators and rode enough of the one hundred Metro miles to confirm the view that the capital city below the ground is as absorbing as it is on the surface.

The Metro is a cameraman's paradise. Lorena photographed the statues and the inlaid ceilings, the tiled floors with their intricate patterns, the ingenious lighting fixtures and the artistically modern chandeliers. She was given permission to shoot the interior of a new subway car, dazzlingly clean and as comfortable as any subway coach can possibly be. She took pictures of the people who posed unsmilingly amidst the unbelievable quiet of the subway traffic. She rode the escalator with her open camera and was allowed to use a flash, despite a general standing rule to the contrary.

But our major interest was religion in this capital of an irreligious state. There were more than a thousand houses of worship in Moscow when Napoleon called the city "holy." We found less than sixty. A hundred years ago the population of Moscow was about 1,000,000; today it is 5,500,000.

In the days of tsarist rule, the Church was so powerful that a Romanov was required to wear the lowly garb of a deacon when receiving the Holy Eucharist. Today no Russian ruler could be persuaded to partake of the sacrament even if it were served to him on a golden platter inside the Kremlin walls.

On Palm Sunday, in the days when the Church ruled Russia, the tsar, bearing a palm branch in one hand, led the horse upon which the patriarch sat playing the role of Christ. Today no ruling Communist would so much as raise his hand in recognition of the symbolism here involved.

I had speculated on these contrasts many times and in Moscow my thoughts on Russian religion were by no means conclusive. On my very first day in the city I met a Moslem imam. I told him of my visit to the mosque in Leningrad close by the Museum of the Great October Revolution. He knew the place. It seemed significant to him that the mosque should be so located, for it was Lenin, father of the Revolution, who, after the oppression and looting by the tsars, urged the Islamic people of Russia to rebuild their houses of worship and reaffirm their faith.

"But," I queried, "has it been possible for you to reaffirm your faith under Soviet rule?"

He looked at me for a studied moment and then exclaimed, "Why, of course!"

Again I wondered whether this was honest conviction or simply fear of the frightful force and ruthless character of the Red regime.

"Isn't it true," I asked, "that the Communists, after promising not to hinder the propagation of your faith, ordered the unveiling of Moslem women and tried to communize your people with atheistic views?"

"Things change," demurred the imam in a voice of noncommittal. "Things change all over the world."

I told him I had been informed that the Communists forbade Moslems to fast during the sacred Islamic month of Ramadan. Fasting, said the Party, weakened the factory workers so that they could not satisfactorily do their jobs.

The imam evaded the point of all this by saying, "We observe our holy Ramadan. Of course, we do."

Like every other cleric, this Moslem minister had only friendly phrases for the Soviets. Yet I had the feeling that deep down in his heart he wanted to say, "The people of Allah are fighting for their lives!" But he did not say it and any such perception on my part was again purely intuitional; and in Russia, particularly in Moscow, I was beginning to doubt even my intuition.

Could I ever arrive at a final appraisal of religion in the U.S.S.R.? Was it true that "we worship as we wish and preach what we please?" Or was freedom of conscience and freedom of religious expression carefully rationed out by the government just as is freedom of the press and freedom of assembly? Is the church's future relentlessly held in the Kremlin's iron hand?

In Moscow a series of events gave me a clearer insight into all this than I had been able to find elsewhere along the way. For instance, late one afternoon I walked around to a Russian Orthodox church a few blocks from my hotel. The huge black doors were locked, but in the churchyard an elderly woman was busily making flower arrangements with affectionate care. I indicated my desire to get inside the church and she escorted me to a side entrance.

Making my way to the foyer, I found the reason for the locked doors. It was clean-up time in the house of God. The sole occupants were a number of charwomen, a photo-genic group if I ever saw one, and I would have given a lot to have had Lorena with me. A wrinkled, explosively fat woman, her cherubic face framed by a white scarf, was reverently polishing a candelabra. Her attitude was one of absolute bliss. Whoever made this candelabra, centuries ago, could have had no greater sense of achievement than did this woman with the scrap of cloth.

A short distance from her was a chubby *matushka* swishing a mop round and round in a pool of dirty water. Her crimson and white head-covering, together with the long black skirt sweeping about her feet, made her look like a puppet which now and again raised its eyes for an ecstatic glimpse at a Madonna high overhead. A younger woman was gouging the hardened tallow out of the candle-holders and another girl was fervently putting a high gloss on a saint in his icon. Other daughters of Martha were cleaning sacred items in a far corner of the church. Intermittently they made the sign of the cross and, bowing low, let it be known that this was their hour for being acolytes as well as laborers in the temple.

I was absorbed in the scene when a young, bearded priest came in. He looked at me as if to say he had been told a stranger had gotten in, but soon he was smiling, as I was, at the ardor of the women and the fascination of the scene.

With meaningful emphasis he laboriously picked an English word. "Tomorrow," he said. "Tomorrow, many people."

"Yes," I agreed. "All will be scrubbed and ready."

"Tomorrow," he repeated and his eyes had a knowing look of promise.

"Russia's tomorrow?" I questioned.

"The church's tomorrow," he managed to say.

His words were a sentimental symbol and perhaps not wholly in conformity with reason. But they told a story in

173

a setting I would long remember. As far as the faithful were concerned, their devotion was sure and their hope confident. "Tomorrow" the worshipers would return. "Tomorrow" the church would once more triumph.

I may have read too much into his words. The scene may not have been an honest preview of things to come, but it seemed like something of an answer. Could it be that throughout Russia, religion was making its subtle concession to the government in the hope of eventually overthrowing its "liberators"?

The following day I met a young Muscovite wearing the red jacket of a Protestant denominational school, Spurgeon College in England. He was a student there and had returned home for a short vacation. I asked him about the church's tomorrow and how he expected to win the atheistic Russians back to Christianity.

"We must witness!" he exclaimed. "Many of our people are doing just that. They are testifying for Christ, not only by speaking, but by living the life. Oh, they speak about Him, too, while they work and whenever they meet someone who is ready for the message."

"Is this permissible?"

His answer was, "We have as much religious liberty as we dare to take."

He meant it. He was one of the most outspoken and evangelistically minded men I had met. This was Russia, but this was also Moscow, and Moscow's religious enthusiasts were looking forward to tomorrow.

In Moscow the religious scene began to make sense. Gradually I had the feeling that my questions were being answered. I found a Roman Catholic church and attended early Mass. I visited a Jewish synagogue where the scrolls of the Torah were being read. I went around to the mosque where the Moslem faithful knelt in prayer. I met several Mennonites and Seventh Day Adventists and one Jehovah's Witness. They were all waiting for "tomorrow" and looking forward to the morning. They all told me, in effect, that religion is up to the people and that while Russia may be a laboratory for atheism, it is even more a laboratory for faith the like of which has not been found on earth since the days of Caesar.

The question these religious leaders are asking, "How fervently do people actually *want* religion?" was being answered with a question from the masses, "What do you have to give us?" This lack of rapport is certainly part of the impasse that exists between organized religion and the proletariat. In a way it is not too different from the situation in our own country where some 70 million Americans are not identified with any church and are frequently asking, "What can institutionalized religion do for me, and under the circumstances what, if anything, can I do for it?"

And this, it seemed to me in Moscow, is how things stand, with the overpowering, outspoken voice of Marxism speaking a bit more clearly than either preachers or the proletariat.

"Religion," said Communism's founder, "is man's consciousness and awareness of himself when he has either not come into his own, or has lost himself. . . . Religious misery is both the expression of real misery and a protest against real misery. Religion is the sigh of the oppressed creature, the temper of a heartless world, as it is the spirit of inanimate circumstances. It is the people's opium."

This bothersome phrase, "the people's opium," is shrugged off by most churchmen. As they look forward to tomorrow they are thinking in terms of present co-existence with Marxists. What else can be done? In Moscow I was asked again and again whether we in America are not also divided between those who go to church and those who do not. When I said that we never gave this distinction much thought, they said neither did they! Unlike any of us who might hold the view, they did not foresee a period when all men would turn to God. As church-goers and non-church-goers work together in America, so church-goers and Marxists work together in Russia. This, they said, is what Americans did not, or would not, understand.

There were also those here in the capital city of the Soviets who expected the religion of the future to be centered strongly in "a Church purified, endowed with authority, a pure theocratic authority, the authority of God invested in consecrated men of God."

I met one of these "men of God" in the person of Metropolitan Nikolai. He is a powerful influence in Russian Orthodoxy, especially in the work that is going forward to bring schismatic churches of Russia and other lands into the Orthodox fold. Supported by his superior, Patriarch Alexei, Nikolai has been emphatically outspoken about "freedom and peace" and how these goals are being obstructed by the West.

He once referred to the United States as a country where "people are lynched, where children are kidnapped, where tear bombs are thrown among the workers . . . where bread is burned before the eyes of the famished . . . where those who attempt to give the term 'freedom' its authentic meaning are thrown into prisons, where gold is used for the bribing of those abroad . . . where there is freedom to steal, to subjugate and to kill."

176

These were his words some ten years ago and it may be that he has changed his opinion through the years. At any rate, I first met him at a mid-afternoon reception at the U.S. Embassy. It was a July 4th observance and the Metropolitan had dropped around to pay his respects. When I first caught sight of him in a crowded room, he was holding out his hand so that an Anglican priest from America could bend his head low over it and perhaps touch it with his lips. Incidentally, the Orthodox Church has assured the Anglican communion that it would welcome it into its unity and would happily recognize the validity of Anglican orders.

Nikolai stood tall and picturesque in the full robes of his high office, his golden cross catching and reflecting shafts of light, his somber, brooding face beneath his gleaming miter reminiscent of tales of ecclesiasticism in tsarist days. Like all who wear the robes of sacrosanct offices, the Metropolitan is insulated against the public. He is neither annoyed nor shocked at emulation. But on this occasion and at a subsequent meeting, he was gracious and generous with me, especially in answering my questions about the progress of religion in Russia.

We could rest assured, he insisted, that church and state were harmoniously working together without "interference one from the other." Technically, the government has two councils. The first, the Council on Orthodox Church Affairs, was created by the government in 1943, the year that marked special Easter celebrations, even the lifting of the curfew and the observance of midnight services. Much of this was in recognition of the Church's contribution to the government's struggle against Hitler's *Wehrmacht*. The Council was designed to clarify relations between Orthodoxy and Communism, to deal with laws relevant to Church affairs, and to supervise the execution of these laws.

The second Council set up by the government carries the ominous-sounding title of Council for the Affairs of Religious Cults. This is a five-man liaison body between the Kremlin and non-Orthodox churches. It is an "assistance council" designed to help churches in the procurement of material for church improvement and worship, to assist in matters dealing with public relations, and to aid in locating and planning new church groups.

I was informed that when twenty or more people gather together and affirm their intention of starting a new church, one would very likely be forthcoming. The group would appeal to the respective Council and the machinery for establishing a place of worship would be set in motion. The whole thing sounded incredibly easy.

And in Moscow I was frequently reminded that the governmental lifting of church restrictions during the critical years of the war was not forgotten. During Holy Week when Moscow was in a state of siege, the Metropolitan Nikolai urged the parishes to ensure the strictest observance of all nighttime regulations. But he was also urging the government to permit the people the utmost opportunity for worship. When news came that the Commandant of Moscow had decided to allow the citizens freedom of movement and freedom to worship, a grateful Orthdox public praised both Church leaders and state officials.

"Our joy knew no bounds," one of the faithful related. "Everyone with one voice expressed thanks and, with peaceful and singing hearts, prepared for the Easter festival. Streams of people could be seen carrying little bundles in their hands. These were little parcels carefully tied in spotless white napkins and tablecloths. They were the traditional *kulich* and *paskha* [Easter cakes]. I asked an old woman, 'Are you going to church, Grandma?' 'Yes, I am going to have the *paskha* blest,' she replied. 'Have you heard the new order that has gone out? May God bless the Soviet authorities. Go about the town without fear, it says, and do what is customary at Easter time. No one will interfere with you!' "

Young people who had never been inside a church, teen-agers who were born after the war, had been told about the government's "kindness" to the Church during the fateful days of the German siege. They were convinced their leaders had always done right by the old people who still "needed religion."

One of these young Russians, a girl employed in a Moscow hotel, who had helped me in the major task of locating a telephone directory, was dead sure that religion as an institutionalized force was dying out. "When the old people are gone, the Church will be gone as well," was her prediction.

We talked about religion at great length. Her English was excellent and she said she was constantly reading English authors. I told her I would send her one of my books.

"Books will never convert me to God," she said with a laugh. "But if you have found in Him something to believe, and if you believe it enough to write about it, that is good."

One evening when she sat at her desk smoothing out and counting a stack of crumpled rubles, I called her a "typical American capitalist." She buried her head in her hands and laughed uproariously. A girl at a nearby desk wanted to know what I had said. The words were relayed and passed around until everyone in the room was laughing heartily and reminding me that for any Russian to be a capitalist was something so preposterous it could lend itself only to comedy. The girl said, "If you knew what we think of your primitive capitalistic system, you would know how funny this is!"

Later she explained that God and capitalism are contradictory. She said, "If God *is*, He is whatever is good. And everyone knows that capitalism is bad." In subsequent talks with her the question of who and what God might conceivably be came up again and again. She was interested in religion, but careful not to betray this interest to her associates.

Travelers in Russia often refer to this growing inquisitiveness among young people as a sure sign of a religious revival. I never found it sufficiently widespread to give cause or hope for such optimism. Far from it. Nonetheless, it is an indication that the quest for God has not been sublimated into the search for national greatness or into the program for a revolutionary social order.

Young Russians talked about this unsatisfied "spiritual" hunger more freely in Moscow than elsewhere. A distinction was always made, however, between religion and "church religion." Whenever Lorena and I met evenings, having gone our separate ways during the day, we exchanged impressions, and we usually came by our own separate routes to the conclusion that here in this showcase city there is a very real conflict in these young Russians, a conflict between an atheistic mind and a spiritually inclined heart.

The fact that Lorena and I often went out separately

had its disadvantages, too. Especially when I visited Zagorsk. I went without her to the famous Troitsa-Sergieva monastery on a day when the churches were crowded with pilgrims and the air was filled with song. Here, some forty miles from Moscow, was a panorama of Russian Orthodoxy such as I had often imagined. Processions of visitors of all classes roamed the grounds while the inscrutable hooded monks moved among them like a pageant out of the tsarist past. Bells were ringing, candles were burning, royally robed dignitaries overawed the crowds, and beggars, mostly aged women, had a field day of almsgetting.

I inquired whether this was a special holy day and was told that every day at Troitsa is holy. You can come here any time, I was assured, and find thousands coming and going in and out of the huge archway cut into the twenty-foot-thick walls.

This is the "Mecca" of Russian Orthodoxy, the native "Jerusalem" of the Eastern Church. It is Moscow's "Pecher-skaya," holding the blessed remains of the Church's most hallowed saint, Sergius, the nobleman who became a monk. Today his body lies in a silver casket and those who chant and pray around the sarcophagus do so with childlike faith. They come as did Princess Sophia, wife of Ivan the Great. She came on foot as does every true child of the church. She came to pray at the grave of the Saint in the hope of obtaining a son. Sergius appeared to her in a vision, then "thrust a male child into her bosom, and it was born nine months later."

Ivan the Terrible walked from Moscow to Troitsa praising God. So did Tsaritsa Maria and Catherine II and many more. When I stood on top of the encircling mile-long wall and looked into the maze of domes and cupolae, museums, monasteries and the archiepiscopal palace, and when the chanting rose from the cathedral, I forgot for the moment that this was Russia. It might easily have been Rome.

According to tradition anyone who comes to Troitsa will have a vision. With Sergius, the Saint, nothing is impossible. He retreated to this spot in 1342 when it was just a wilderness with only a lonely hermitage. He built a chapel with his own hands and called it the "Source of Life." The faithful say the chapel has always lived up to its name. They are convinced that the destiny of Russia is foreshadowed by the destiny of Troitsa at Zagorsk and that a nation's tomorrow can be judged by what transpires here today.

So it has always been, they will tell you. In 1609 the monastery withstood a sixteen-month siege by the Poles. Later, when Moscow fell under Polish rule, the nucleus of resistance was again formed at Troitsa and Holy Mother Moscow was liberated. In the monastery of Troitsa the brother-tsars, Ivan and Peter, found refuge from the Strelitzes, and here Peter the Great outlined many of his campaigns and strategies.

There are items at Zagorsk which can never be bought and there are also items for sale. Among the first are priceless robes and jewels and, it is said, more precious pearls than in all of Europe. Among the second were some ancient icons which put my "Rublev" to shame. I bargained with the bearded monk in charge of these treasures and found one for three hundred rubles that I desperately wanted. I had nothing but traveler's checks—American— and here they could not be converted into coin of the realm. My interpreter and I tried our best to negotiate a purchase, but it was impossible. This *was* Russia. Neither monks nor priest nor Sergius himself was able to help me. The only thing I got out of the conversations was a proverb, "Americans either carry too much money or not enough. It is always that way with the capitalistic imperialists."

Even so, I loved Troitsa, and it is one place I would love to revisit. I felt a sense of freedom there, almost of the kind we know in America. When I visited with several of the monastery officials, when I heard their enthusiasm for the young men who are preparing for the priesthood here, and especially when I took pictures of several smiling monks with my Polaroid, I felt a wholesomeness about Russian religion that I had not experienced elsewhere. If the teacher in Stalingrad believed the immortal dead were praying along the Volga, certainly they were walking and talking to us in Zagorsk. Even the children romping on the grounds that day seemed almost to be hearing a friendly voice saying, "Let them come unto Me."

The good, rich feeling of the day at Troitsa went back to Moscow with us. Our cabbie was speeding along at a good pace when suddenly he made a low, disgruntled outcry. He had caught sight of a motorcycle cop in his rearview mirror. We looked back and my interpreter with good American inflection exclaimed, "Boy-o-boy!"

Caught for speeding in Russia, I thought. What now? And with nothing but traveler's checks. We pulled off the road and in a moment the cop was sauntering up to our car with casual authority.

The questions are the same all over the world. "What's the hurry? Do you know how fast you were going? Your driver's license? Of course, you know the speed in this zone?"

The answers were the same, too, with a courteous, *"Da, Tovarish,"* (Yes, Comrade) tacked on to every one of them. Then the driver's license and the taxi were given another appraisal and the officer threw me an inquiring glance. My interpreter-friend spoke charmingly in Russian and out of his words I caught "Amerikanski" and "Zagorsk" and enough to understand why the cop nodded, touched his finger to his cap, told the driver, in effect, to "Watch it next time," and strolled off.

As we resumed our trip, my interpreter leaned back casually and said, "There was nothing to worry about. Our police are always very courteous. Very courteous, as you saw. By the way, do you have a cigarette?"

From here the conversation turned back to the U.S.A. and questions as to how traffic officers handle things in our country. Soon I was being interrogated, as I had often been elsewhere in Russia, about the national temper of the American people, the characteristic traits which the Soviet press has often said are molded in hate and racism, and fired in atrocities and crime.

This, of course, led most logically to the inevitable topic of war and peace. We could never get away from it, for it cannot be said often enough that the Communist peace offensive has been tremendously effective among its own people. We Americans have been made to live in the minds of the Russians as imperialistic aggressors. From all the propaganda which the Russian populace has heard, God and the Soviets are made to appear as closer partners in the cause for peace than God and the Americans can ever be. Books, pamphlets and the daily talk of individuals on the subject of peaceful intentions invariably begin with a statement to the effect that "the people of the Soviet

Union unanimously want peace and that is why we are so profoundly alarmed at the testing of bombs and missiles by the United States."

Wherever I went, whether to a meeting in a cathedral or a taxi to Zagorsk, I was told that nowhere in the world is any country working as fervently at establishing "good will among men" as is Russia. I was informed that the program was centered in a World Council of Peace which had an affiliated office in Moscow called the Soviet Peace Committee. Russian clerics had often suggested that I drop in at this office and discover for myself how earnestly the work is progressing.

Tass, the official Soviet news agency, was telling the Russian people that years ago, in late March, 1949, the "United States Peace Congress" got off to a great start only to be boycotted by reactionary "imperialistic forces and Wall Street warmongers." The reference, of course, was to the "Cultural and Scientific Conference for World Peace" which was held in New York at the Waldorf-Astoria and closed with a mass meeting in Madison Square Garden. It was, as I recalled from American news reports, anything but a peaceful meeting. Shostakovich was there. So was the Polish author Kruczkowski, the Cuban poet Guilien, the British philosopher William Olaf Stapledon, and other scientific and cultural figures from various foreign countries as well as from the United States.

At the time our State Department said that the meeting was packed with Communists and that it was nothing more than a sounding board for Communist propaganda. Many other Americans felt the same way about it. Two thousand banner-carrying pickets paraded the streets in front of the Garden whenever meetings were held. They brandished signs reading, "Russians, go home!" "Free Cardinal Minds-zenty!" "You're too red for us!" To add to the confusion and travail of the birth of this "Peace Congress," federal agents seized three Canadian delegates for alleged Communist activities. A rival meeting under the heading of "Americans for Intellectual Freedom" was staged in New York at the same time, one of its leading figures being Alexander Kerensky, who had been president of the Provisional Government of Russia after the fall of the tsar.

All in all, the attempt at creating an international movement for peace resulted in a stormy session and about the only memorable feature that came out of it was a statement by one participant summarizing the results of the Conference: "No one in the U.S.S.R. wants war with the U.S., but many in the U.S.S.R. fear American capitalism and hope it will be destroyed. No one in the U.S. wants war with the U.S.S.R., but many in the U.S. fear Russian socialism and hope it will be destroyed."

The Soviet press reported to the Russian people that since the United States Peace Congress had been "sacked," it was up to the Soviets to see it through. It repeated the claim that the most emphatic advocates and workers for peace were the members of the Soviet delegation. It was Russia's A. A. Fadeyev who told the delegates, "It is almost impossible to find one unbiased American or Western European who, after setting foot on our soil, does not feel the healthy, peaceful pulse of life in the whole atmosphere of our country."

I did not feel it quite that strongly. My reaction to Russia's "will for peace" was not quite so vivid. But surely the organization for peace—peace as a concept regardless of peace as a workable reality—was very much in evidence.

I realized that ever since the start of our trip we had been reminded in signs and banners of *"Mir i Druzhba!"* (Peace and Friendship). A Hindu whom I met in Moscow told me his country was convinced that Russia wanted peace more sincerely than did America. The World Council of Peace had made it clear that it was compelled to drop the United States and reorient itself entirely toward the eastern world.

This was obvious from reports in *Pravda* and *Izvestia*. They declared that, through the years, 117,669,320 Soviet citizens had signed an appeal for the conclusion of a peace pact among the five great powers, the U.S.A., U.S.S.R., Chinese People's Republic, Britain, and France. They accused the U.S.A., Britain, and France of "craving a new war and making mad preparations for it." They said, "A handful of billionaires and millionaires need a new war to acquire super-profits, and to plunder other countries."

Obviously, said *Pravda*, the U.S.S.R. and the Chinese People's Republic must go it alone. The United States, it declared, believes that the existence of the United Nations and its charter makes a peace pact superfluous. American people are not free to choose peace even if they desire it, said *Tass*. A report from the Moscow patriarchate was equally bitter, "Capitalism needs and cherishes only a religion which propagandizes and strengthens and elucidates its dominant role in the state. . . . The most tested and faithful servant of capitalism is the Vatican which is turning more and more to America and the West."

With all of this as a background, I went without the benefit of interpreter or Intourist guide to 10 Kropotkin Street where the Soviet Peace Committee has its headquarters. Two flights up I found spacious offices, an assembly hall and a directors' room where I was greeted by secretary Mikhail Kotov. He summoned two other men, one of whom spoke English very well, and asked me why I had come, and where I had heard about the Committee. When I explained that I had been touring Russia because of my interest in religion, that my field was religious research, they showed great interest.

"Tell us," exclaimed Mr. Kotov, "why is America opposed to peace? Why are American churches afraid to cooperate with the World Council of Peace? You know, of course, that not a single representative of American churches attended our meeting in Ceylon. Why, why, *why* cannot a bridge of understanding be built between our two great nations?"

His voice rose with emotion. The interpreter also spoke with a passion I had not heard anywhere else, not even among the most devoted clergymen. I was given a briefing on the special sessions of the World Council of Peace. I was handed excerpts and quotations from the resolutions and recommendations. I was shown that at a meeting in Helsinki, the "whole world was there" with the exception of the United States.

"The World Council of Peace," I was assured, "is the highest expression of the forces of peace which have succeeded in preventing the unleashing of a new world war. But they must now dispel the *threat* of war that hangs over mankind. Atomic and thermonuclear bombs hang by a thread over the heads of men, women and children. Peace is indispensable. Peace is the greatest need. Peace is the prerequisite for the development of man's creative powers."

I have been in revival meetings in many parts of the

world and I have spoken to religious enthusiasts in many nations. These men of the Soviet Peace Committee were bursting with a zeal which, self-generated or not, was almost charismatic. They were evangelists for peace, and they sounded like many of our high-powered radio preachers. They talked to me as if it had been years since anyone from America had dropped in on them. I felt they truly wanted friendship with our country. Their ways might not be our ways, their motives might be open to suspicion, but these men surely had a job to do—to sell the world the feeling that Russia sincerely wants to dispel distrust. I felt that I was among crusaders, fiery crusaders for their cause.

What is a person to say under these circumstances? I was torn by an inner conflict. Should I have said, "Well, gentlemen, we do not trust you. Yours is a government of broken promises. We have reason to believe that your overtures to us in behalf of peace are deceptive. You will have to convince us that you are acting in good faith and have no sinister motivation."

I could have expressed other suspicions and fears. Communism *does* have a philosophy of world conquest. It *has* been known to incite war while deploring it. It *is* committed to the proposition that the individual is of less importance than the state. It could be that this office is only a façade behind which there is a lurking terror. How is a man to know? Who has the genius and the insight to judge these movements wisely and without prejudice, yet not naively and with too much trust? As I sat at the table with these men, I felt that never had there been a time or a place in history that required greater understanding. For it was, of course, part of my belief that the world *could* be saved, and would indeed *need* to be saved, through religious faith.

Statistics flashed through my mind. What if all the religious people in the world *could* unite for peace, not in any attempt at uniformity or ecclesiastical conformity, but simply for the sake of creating a few solid years in which men could have a chance to live without fear, and work without threat of war? There are nearly 500 million Roman Catholics in the world, nearly 250 million Protestants, and about 130 million Eastern Orthodox. There are 400 million Moslems, 320 million Hindus, 300 million Confucianists, 150 million Buddhists. Nearly all of the 2,600 million people in the world worship God, or some sort of god. Who among them does not desire peace?

My thoughts swept around the globe to temples, mosques, cathedrals, churches and shrines, but they always came back to Russia and this room, and to our suspicions, not of the Russian people, but of the Communist regime. We can love the Russian masses with Christian compassion, but what shall we do about the Communist plot? We can love the churches of Russia, too, but what can we do with the statement of the Moscow patriarchate which declared, "The Church regards with the greatest respect and the warmest appreciation the Soviet Government which expresses the will of the people and is constantly concerned for the welfare of the people."

I remembered the report of American churchmen, nine of them, who, after a visit to Russia, stated, "We are convinced that the Russian churches and people ardently desire peace. However, the World Peace Council has consistently taken the same line as that of the Soviet Government, namely, that participants from the West have not been truly representative of Western churches. We emphasized the necessity of finding some bases other than their past positions if we are to work together for peace. We made it clear that the means to peace are as important as the end."

The impasse is crystal clear. We say that we are suspicious of the World Council of Peace, and the Russians tell us that they are suspicious of the World Council of Churches which the churchmen represent. We say, "We want peace"; the Russians say, "We want peace"; the whole religious world is saying, "We want peace"; and everyone, it seems, is ready to fight to prove it.

It is a deadlock. The usual polemics are blocking all moves. We insist that Soviet beliefs make the scientific quest for objectivity impossible. They say that we are wrapped in our own subjective self-righteousness. We tell them that, according to their teaching, the individual is of less importance than the state. They retaliate by insisting that we are ambitiously trying to save our churchianity. We politely inform them that they have formally rejected the Fatherhood of God. They shoot back that we have just as formally denied Him by our refusal to cooperate in the Brotherhood of Man.

The thing that bothered me most, as I sat through these two hours of excited and heated pleas for peace, was that we in America could not seem to negotiate with the Russians without the support of A-bombs and missiles and satellites. As Christians, we may not wish to follow the pattern of Communism and bargain against a background of power and threats of our ability to retaliate and annihilate, but can we do otherwise? Do we have the courage and the wisdom to do otherwise? Can we "conquer" the world as

Jesus did, without force? This was His genius, but is it ours?

Whether the World Council of Peace is a plot or the reflection of an honest hope, whether the American churches are right or wrong in rejecting the pleas of the Soviet Peace Committee, one thing is sure: the people of the world are sick and tired of war. They are fed up with burying their dead in the futility and waste of a struggle for power. They are determined to live without fear, and if religion cannot or will not help them achieve this end, they will look for help elsewhere, wherever it can be found. But where else *can* it be found?

I thought of this especially when the secretary seized both my hands in his and, with burning Russian aggressiveness, pleaded with me to investigate more thoroughly their documents and resolutions so that I could see for myself how sincere they are. I said to myself exactly what many another American would have said: If these men are sincere, we should talk to them again. If they are not, let's call their bluff. Let's start our own peace offensive and show the world how unitedly we Christians of America can stand together in this tremendous cause! What if our churches should suddenly march together, signifying that the brotherhood we hope to achieve in the world has been first achieved at home?

These thoughts came to me as I stood in the offices of the Soviet Peace Committee. Here we were, each waiting for the dawn, each trying to convince the other that his country was the more ambitious for peace.

A bit of wry American humor came to my mind, too. I could not help thinking, even while the secretary held my hands warmly in his, that it might not be long before we would again be shaking our fists at each other across the Atlantic! Such is the fallibility of man; and that, it seemed to me more strongly than ever before, is why we so desperately need the help and grace of God.

That was why I had to say, "Gentlemen, we'll never be able to do it alone."

8. Russia's Challenge
to America's Faith

IN MY ATTEMPT to learn about religion in Russia, I discovered a challenge, not a threat, to religion all over the world and more particularly to religion in America. The challenge is that we must live our faith as never before, define it to a degree never before thought necessary, and examine it anew in the light of honesty and truth. For, whether we asked for it or not, we have the reputation of being the most religious nation on earth.

Perhaps we have asked for it. We have published high-powered statistics about our spiritual strength as measured in church building programs, church membership, church finances. We have organized a campaign to erect a string of churches along the edge of the Iron Curtain so that we might impress the Russians with the need for our type of religious faith. We have said that since Russia is godless, its people must be evil; and Christian churchmen have voiced the threat that God in His wrath will ultimately destroy the Soviet state.

Our reputation for being the most religious nation on

earth is part of the price we have paid for sending evangelists and missionaries around the world to proselytize and convert, and for sending teams of clergymen to the U.S.S.R. to appraise the worth of Russian faith. We are foremost among those carrying out the Great Commission to "teach all nations" (Matt. 28:19).

Some Russians consider even our aid to foreign countries a token of our feeling of religious superiority. They say we are priding ourselves about our religion every time we testify to the great things God has done for us. Good men should not boast about their goodness, they said to me, nor should anyone stand up in public and preach that his way of life is the one and only way.

Christ may have given the keys of heaven and hell to the Roman Catholic Church, but Russians do not believe it. God may have imparted a specific plan of salvation to the Protestants, but the self-termed atheists are skeptical. America may be the home of those whom God has chosen for special favors, but the Reds are out to challenge the claim.

We are dealing with a type of mind, the Marxist mind, which demands objective practice as the criterion of truth, asks us to make good on what we proclaim, and to carry out the principles we volubly profess. Actually, this kind of thinking may be a good thing for us. We may need to be awakened spiritually as we were rudely awakened scientifically when the first Russian satellites cut their orbits across the sky.

My first impulse, when Russians insinuated that we boasted about our religion, was to ask whether Communism was not also a boast. I started to say that if they are out to Communize the world, why should they blame us for wishing to Christianize it? Don't they assume superiority every time they call attention to the advantages of their system and the glory of their work? Isn't it as much or more of a boast for them to deny God as it is for us to declare Him? Is it not as presumptuous for them to contend that man's social existence determines his consciousness as it is for us to argue that man's consciousness determines his existence?

I quickly realized that a defensive attitude leads nowhere. We could go on forever insisting that we are right and they are wrong; and they no doubt would be willing to stay with us insisting that we're wrong and they're right.

Rather than continuing to defend our position or to condemn theirs, I decided to stay as close as possible to the pursuit of my original question, the question that had lured me to Russia: can the religious impulse be sublimated into that which is not religious? I came to Russia, as I have said, with the oft-tested belief that wherever man lives, man worships. I believed with all my heart that man is by nature spiritual.

But in Russia life is lived in the pattern of mass movement. The Kremlin wants us to believe that the idea of an individual embarking on a personal spiritual quest is inconceivable. Such a spectacle—that of a man seeking God—is in itself a form of private enterprise and should be discouraged!

I could say that the Communists affirmed the existence of God by their denial of Him, falling back upon the old argument that we need not deny that which does not exist. But Communism insists that we must deny even the *illusion* of God. God, they ruthlessly contend, is a fabrication, a lie, along with other such lies as Satan and St. Nick. Over and over I had to remind myself that to the Marxist all reality is material. Truth to him is identified with matter. Mind is matter. Principle, honesty, conduct are all based on matter. To be a Marxist is to discover and acknowledge truth only through sense perception, never by way of spiritual insight.

But, having said all that, what conclusions had I actually reached? What answers had I found in this laboratory of unbelief? A few things could be said with certainty: Russians cannot be lumped together as though they are all integral parts of a Communist block; not all Communists are confirmed atheists; nor are all atheists malevolent. This is important in its direct bearing upon an American psychosis which has identified non-church members, even in America, with atheism and, therefore, with Communism. The 70 million Americans whose names do not appear on church roles are sometimes adjudged irreligious because of it. They should not be so judged. Their lack of interest in institutionalized religion should not be construed as a sign of spiritual unbelief, nor should unbelief be considered analogous to Communism.

An unbeliever, anywhere in the world, need not necessarily be a Communist. But in Russia, the majority of the 7 million "card-carrying" Communists are affirmed atheists. No church member holds either a responsible government position or one of economic leadership. And no true Communist is a church member. All subscribe to an anti-God, anti-Christ policy, and yet, what these millions actually *believe* about God is anyone's guess.

A full-fledged Communist said to me, "What I believe about religion is my business. Maybe I believe in God, and maybe I do not. The only thing the party wants to know is whether or not I belong to a church. I do not belong to a church. But what I believe and think about religion belongs to me."

When I asked another what he would consider the ideal church, if churches there must be, he said, "A place where people gather to sing together, and to pray separately."

Communism clearly states that religion is a private matter until it takes the form of an organization, or of an institution. Then it becomes a public concern. Organization implies a clash of loyalties.

The Bolsheviks insisted that the workers needed protection against the intrigue and exploitation of the Church no less than against the oppression of the landowning and capitalistic classes. The Party was heralded as a united front against "economic injustice" and "religious deception." Lenin said, "The class-conscious worker of today leaves heaven to the priests and bourgeois hypocrites. He fights for a better life for himself, here on earth."

Lenin, president of the Soviets from 1917 to 1924, had no such slogans as, "Down with religion!" or "Long live atheism!" He was too clever for that. He declared that the planned propagation of atheism is injurious to the class struggle.

"The anarchist who preaches against God at all costs," he told his followers, "actually helps the priests and the bourgeoisie. The Marxist must be a dialectical materialist, one who fights against religion not by abstract, purely theoretical propaganda, but concretely on the basis of the class struggle . . . a struggle which will educate the masses better than anything else can do."

This is the current Communist approach. Compared with the closing of churches, persecution of ministers, and execution of priests in the post-Revolution years, the present state of religion in Russia is one of relative freedom and peace. It is not freedom as we know it in the United States. While there is official separation of Church and State, and though non-Communists may freely belong to a church, there are still severe restrictions on the propagation and function of religion in the U.S.S.R. Evangelistic crusades, young people's meetings, laymen's movements, Sunday schools and parochial schools are generally forbidden. Freedom of worship is confined to the privilege of attending church services and choir rehearsals.

Several priests and ministers told me they believe that more restriction will be lifted and the situation will continue to improve. They felt that as Russia's prestige and power grow abroad, more and more concessions will be made at home. Though the Kremlin leaders may appear ruthless and despotic, they have, as I was told by the teacher in Stalingrad, a listening ear directed toward public opinion and world reaction.

The Kremlin leaders want Russia to be the world's number-one nation. Everything from agriculture to missiles is in contest, and the power of religion, or the lack of it, is a major issue in which the winning of the world opinion is part of the prize. They are wise enough to know that if they can win the minds of men through impressive scientific achievements, they may win the souls of men by a gradual transition from atheistic Communism to agnostic Communism. This is part of their challenge.

Challenging, too, were the question of young Russians when they asked, "In what way does religion make Americans different from us? Don't most Americans feel that by professing morality they are practicing morality? Are

Americans who attend church higher-principled than those who do not attend?"

Questions like these are in the minds of Russian students, 90 per cent of whom have never been inside a church, but most of whom are seriously and realistically concerned about basic values in life. They want evidence that what we believe has relevancy in the policies by which we live and act.

Young Russia's preconceived notion that religious people cannot be trusted is as deep-seated as our contention that godless people cannot be good. They have been systematically schooled regarding the sins of which organized religion has, unfortunately, often been guilty. They have not been told about religion's blessings, its help to humanity or its solace to individual lives. They are startlingly uninformed about the contributions of contemporary faith to humanity; most of the young people with whom I talked had never heard of a man called Albert Schweitzer.

By our crime statistics, our juvenile delinquency, our secularism and our "capitalistic imperialism," they judge that religion in the U.S.A. is impotent. They sincerely believe that Communism is less guilty of the sins of racism, immorality, and exploitation than is Christianity. Much of our spiritual force is lost because it is contradicted by our actions.

Communism may never be construed as a religion by the Soviets, but as a way of life it will continue to be defined more and more. It is not at all inconceivable that God, as a Prime Mover in the universe, may one day be defined as a primary "spiritual" principle by the Russian proletariat.

There is already a growing insistence in Communism

that materialistic philosophy is rich in the ethical and moral qualities which religion, particularly Christianity, holds as basic. This may seem contradictory to us, but the fact remains that Communism is challenging those of us who may have doubted that it is impossible to be "good without God."

Despite an enforced atheism, or perhaps because of it, there is a growing awareness among young Russians that they must demonstrate to the world that a man can be "righteous" without religion. They will still have to prove that this *is* possible in the long run, but outspoken humanists contend they are proving it.

I heard frequent references to benevolent Marxists, altruistic freethinkers, beneficent socialists. The popularity of such phrases is being bolstered by the prevailing propaganda that Christianity is divisive, selfish, exploitive. A priest of the Russian Orthodox faith said to me, "We (Russia) may yet have to teach the Western religious world how to work together. We have more cooperation among faiths here than you have in the United States."

We Americans know what our heritage of religious freedom means to us, and what it implies. We know the price at which this heritage was purchased. We know the liberty our faith gives us, the personal dignity it inspires, the responsibility it enjoins, and the goals, unrealized and unattained, that it sets before us. We know the vision of the kingdom of God it presents to us. But Russia evaluates our religiosity by none of these things. It sees us only as a nation, and judges us on the basis of our social and political conduct—our policies, methods, and aims in the struggle for world domination.

Regardless of how you and I feel about it, Russia is convinced that the spiritual voice of America in international affairs is less than a whisper. Money talks, military power talks, prestige talks, but religion has not been able to get in a word, even edgewise. Russia believes there is no united prophetic voice in America, no religious cutting edge, no men of courage who stand for God without thought of personal gain or thought of fame. One Russian grimly referred to our religion as that of "the full stomach and the Cadillac car."

This, too, is part of the challenge.

Many Americans have dreamed of some dramatic move which would utilize and reflect the faith that earnest Christians hold, but, so far it has not been possible to transmit this into a national policy or translate it into action.

Some Americans, especially those belonging to our country's traditional "peace groups," have been urging a halt to the arms race for some time. They are being joined by a growing witness on the part of the church, and the voices of religious leaders are beginning to be heard on the problems and issues of war and peace. Churchmen are coming to realize that it is high time for courageous action in the name of the Christian faith.

Russia is challenging us to define how far we are willing to go in our trust in God. We are bluntly being asked how realistic we can be in living out what our religion proclaims. We are even faced with the necessity of reappraising our values.

Many a young Russian said to me, "I do not miss the things you Americans think you must have to live happily. I have a goal to work for and this means more to me than an easy life."

Such a statement may of course be mere juvenile idealism, yet it *is* idealism and expresses at least one bent of the Russian student mind. It is unrealistic for us not to consider the implications here involved.

On the Christmas following the launching of the Russian satellite, a cartoon appeared in American papers. It showed a burly Communist confronting a young American boy who was pulling a Christmas sled. The Communist was saying, "Look! We have Sputnik!" To which the boy replied, "But no Saint Nik!"

The meaning is clear. No country in the world has the sense of concern, the wish to help and share, which we Americans have. We see clearly the inherent fallacy of Communist thought. We know that the laws which Communism's leaders do not believe in need not be obeyed by them. We believe we have a law higher than the law of the commune or the law of a liberal conscience and we recognize that this higher law is God. The law is there, though we often fall short of attaining it. This striving toward oneness with God, this belief in the possible realization of the fulfillment of man's deepest quest, is our greatest national heritage. We believe that we are able to be better and nobler people than we are, and that in order to achieve these qualities we must be free.

Communism has not been able to satisfy the human desire for freedom and the quest of the spirit, and anyone who meets the Russian people with sympathy and understanding will realize this fact. My Russian journey convinced me that the yearning for God which I had found in other parts of the world is no less real among the Soviet people. It cannot be sublimated into something which is not spiritual.

Accompanying Communistic scientific progress is a growing sense of spiritual loss and spiritual maladjustment.

The individual in the Russian proletariat seeks to discover and complete and transcend himself in Someone and Something higher and greater than nationalism or the goal of a classless world. Neither economic determinism nor dialectical materialism has been able to satisfy man's awareness that life is related to an unseen, eternal Force. The source of this quest is in the very nature of man, and, obviously, it is found in Russians as in everyone else.

Any doubt I might have had about this was dispelled on my final Sunday in Moscow, for it was my privilege that morning to speak from the pulpit of the Moscow Baptist Church, the "fastest-growing church in the world."

Arrangements for my participation in the service were made when I dropped in, unannounced and alone, at the church office on Maly Vuzovsky Lane. The moment I got inside the doors, I realized I was in the heart of a going concern. Secretaries were busily at work, telephones were ringing, and an American, Kirby Page, was talking to an interpreter about a group that he had brought, on tour, from the States.

I was cordially greeted by the two chief pastors of this church who came from behind their cramped and crowded desks to shake my hand. The alert and scholarly Pastor Karev spoke German. The venerable, bearded Pastor Zhidkov seemed to understand all languages as well as the language of the spirit, but he spoke only Russian. I found these men easy to meet, hospitable, and eager to be friendly, though Pastor Karev made it clear, early in our meeting, that he could not for the life of him understand why American churches refused to cooperate in the World Council of Peace.

My research in religion interested these men very much.

They felt that Russia was conducting a successful experiment in inter-religious relations. They saw in Russian religion some of the qualities of the early apostolic church. They realized the need for "witnessing."

They had no criticism of the Kremlin, no remorse about the challenge that confronted the church in Russia, no complaint about anything except that they wished America would trust Russia more—and by "Russia" they meant the people, people like themselves and like the 600,000 members who make up the Evangelical Baptist churches of the Soviet Union. By "America" they meant the people *and* the government because we claim that our government is by and for the people. That is why more is expected of us. Christians must cooperate with other Christians regardless of racial or cultural differences, Pastor Karev said. Russian Christians, he said, are willing to do it, and most Baptists are willing. The Baptist World Alliance, I was told has 21 million members in one hundred countries speaking a hundred different languages and dialects, and among Baptists there are none more deeply committed than the Russian Evangelical Baptists.

I was assured I would meet many of them on Sunday morning. How many? Well, the church could accommodate about nine hundred but at least fourteen hundred would somehow crowd into the service. This would be the ten thirty service and I was advised that throughout Sunday—every Sunday—five services are held, each crowded to the doors with fourteen hundred or more worshipers.

Would Lorena be permitted to take pictures? Of course. Could she be given a vantage point in the balcony? Why not! An American suggested he wanted to put my remarks on tape recording. Would that be allowed? Surely. The only concern in any of these details was that the spirit of worship should not be impaired. Outside of that, freedom was unlimited.

I do not think of myself as a preacher, so I did not plan to deliver a sermon, but what I wanted more than anything else was to bring greetings from America and tell Russians about religion's role in American life. Would that be permissible? The pastors gave me *carte blanche* to say whatever I wished. I was pleased at this because churchmen back home had told me all sorts of weird stories about enforced restrictions. One man, I recalled, insisted that all remarks had to be put down in writing and submitted to the church officials before presentation to the public. This may have been true during the Stalin regime, but it was not true in my experience. I was not told what to say or what not to say. I decided to write out nothing, but to speak extemporaneously "as the spirit moved me."

Before I came to Russia I had heard some stirring things about this Moscow Baptist Church. A year ago an industrialist friend of mine, Vern L. Schield, attended an evening service here. He was surprised when several enthusiastically scrawled notes fluttered down from the balcony overhead. Knowing of my interest in religion, he brought the notes home to me. Written on shreds of white paper in laborious English, they said, "You are quite welcome, dear guests!" "Remember our kind regards to your brothers and sisters in the U.S.A." "We wish you well!" "God be with you!"

The history of the Baptist faith in Russia goes back nearly a hundred years. It began with Martin Kalweit, a Lutheran, who, during a visit to Germany, was greatly impressed with the life and teachings of the German Baptists.

Convinced of the validity of adult baptism, and inspired by the exemplary life of the people he met, he asked to be rebaptized, joined the church and returned to Russia to propagate the faith.

In those days it was against the law to proselytize from the fold of Russian Orthodoxy, but Kalweit's fervor, in keeping with good Baptist doctrine, knew no law but love, no book but the Bible, no creed but Christ. The first convert was a Transcaucasian merchant, Nikita Voronin. Kalweit baptized him in a river and "anointed him with his zeal." With the help of Baptists in England, Canada and America, despised and persecuted by Orthodoxy, the work grew until today as part of the Baptist World Alliance it claims five thousand churches in the U.S.S.R.—and is growing.

I saw how it was growing when Lorena and I came to the services on Sunday morning. At ten o'clock the crowds in front of the church blocked our taxi. At ten fifteen I had the feeling that it was a Christmas or an Easter service. We were told there would be not fourteen hundred but sixteen hundred this morning—not because an American was speaking, but simply because Christ is enthusiastically worshipped at Maly Vuzovsky Lane.

Several young men helped us through the throngs into the church office. Intourist was right. One of the guides had told me, "You will find worshipers there all right!" They were everywhere, old people, young people, well-dressed and poorly dressed people. People were even trying patiently to find places in the hallways, though they would be unable to see the chancel from those positions.

Lorena required the aid of two men to reach her assigned place in the balcony. I caught a glimpse of her later, and how she was able to manipulate her cameras in that crowd I will never know. The balcony, which runs in a semicircle around the auditorium, was filled to dangerous proportions, far beyond its capacity. Stairways were packed. Pews had evidently been occupied immediately after the close of the previous service. People are urged to attend only one service so as to make room for other worshipers for the services that follow. The aisles were jammed in a way that would have shocked any safety-minded American.

The hundreds waiting on the street would never get in for this session. From the church chancel where the pastors and I had arrived by many an *"Izvinite!"* (Pardon me), I could see the hundred-voice choir gathering in the center loft of the balcony. Clarence Westphal, the American who planned to record the singing and my remarks, managed to join us in the chancel. Also present were a woman interpreter, appointed by Dr. Karev, and three scholarly young Russians, studying for the Baptist ministry.

An organ prelude opened the service, and a wave of devotion moved through the congregation. The sea of shawled heads bowed low. Men who stood among the throngs of elderly women lifted their heads proudly. Young people, perhaps two hundred, as nearly as I could estimate their number, became uncommonly reverent. I recalled what a Russian student told me. "It is wrong," he said, "ever to compare Russian young people with the Hitler youth as some people like to do. We have not been indoctrinated with the idea of a super-race. We are not the victims of hate campaigns. We have not been trained for war. We are trained for peace. We are being taught to be good."

These young people, most of them in their early twenties, looked good. Evidently worship meant something to them. Many closed their eyes in prayer during the organ prelude.

I have been in Christian churches in many places and have often been moved by a people's devotion, but for one brief, electrifying moment, I felt a thrill here unlike any I could recall. I was caught for a moment in the thought that worship is more precious where it is not free. A Christian in Russia is God's witness by the very fact of being a Christian. It means something to declare for Christ here under a godless government. At least it means that a man is willing to stand up and be counted.

I was glad I was not asked to speak after the first stirring hymn or following the first pastoral prayer. Though the words were foreign to me, their spirit communicated to me the heart of faith, which is always expressed in sincerity and can be felt, always, as a thing experienced. Religion's most rabid critic and Russia's most severe censor would, I feel sure, have stood in awe at the majesty of the singing and the sincerity of the ministers who opened this service with prayer.

Had I been asked to speak just then I would have been tempted to say that God still walks the Russian streets, still lives in peasants' hearts, still haunts the churches and still speaks to Russian youth. I would have said: He will emerge again in Russia. He will be made known again. He will be proclaimed again in the rich glory of His presence and the knowledge of His love.

It was communion service. The huge loaves of bread and the silver goblets were placed upon the table beneath the pulpit. After the customary scripture readings and the traditional "preparation for the Lord's Supper" which consists of soul-searching questions by the pastor and a confession on the part of the congregation, the elements were administered. Slowly and reverently, twelve elders of the church passed the silver platters among the people. On the platters lay the crumbs of bread which had been blessed by the minister with the familiar words, "This is my body which is broken for you." Then the wine, sanctified under the well-known words, "This cup is my blood of the new covenant," was poured into the large goblets. These were passed among the believers, returned for refilling, then passed again until the time—long, consecrated moments later—when everyone had partaken.

The bread and wine were offered to me also, though I had been told that sometimes "closed communion" is observed and non-members are not served. I accepted the elements with a feeling that took me back to my first Eucharist in our little German church back home, and I stood now, as then, wondering how this sense of oneness with God and with one's fellowmen can be made more enduring and more secure.

Here the fundamental force of Russian atheism was being met head-on by the fundamental force of the Christian faith. The spiritually vigorous Baptists were spelling out their belief as courageously as any organized group would dare to do. God was being worshiped through the mystical body of Christ in a country where, as far as the government is concerned, the name of God, if it should ever be written officially, would not even be capitalized.

It was in the deep and reverent aftermath of the distribution of the bread and wine that Pastor Karev introduced me to the congregation. He made it clear that I had not come at the request of any particular religious denomination; that I was not a governmental representative; that my primary aim was a personal interest in Russian religion. He was always pleased, he said, when the Christians of America, or Christians from anywhere in the world, came to Moscow, and to the church. Whatever I cared to say from the pulpit would, he felt sure, be appreciated.

The young woman, an unusually capable interpreter, stood with me in the pulpit. Quickly and fluently, she transmitted to the ministers and to the people my appreciation of the privilege extended me. I told them, "I wish that every American could have the opportunity to stand here in this pulpit. I wish that my fellow Americans could see this scene, the crowded church and the rows of people standing in the aisles. From here it looks like a living cross. I bring you greetings from America. We feel that better understanding is one of Christianity's great ideals, and the best way we can understand each other is to meet together on a person-to-person basis. World peace is our great challenge and our common goal. I wish to assure you that the people of the United States wish peace very earnestly. They wish to live at peace with all the world."

As this was translated for the congregation, many among them shook their heads sorrowfully. Tears came to the eyes of several of the women. They desperately wished to believe that what their speaker was saying was true. They wished to be reassured about America's desire for peace. They wished, also, to hear of America's selflessness in the aid and charities to which it is committed. They wanted to be told again about America's greatness and goodness in the hope that I might contradict some of the things they had heard to the contrary. Most of all, they wanted to be convinced that Americans did not hate the Russian people, did not look down upon them, did not really wish to blast them off the face of the earth.

I will confess to a bit of sentimentality. I said to them, "I seem to see the face of my mother in many of you women. I remember how often my mother brought the bread for the Lord's Supper in my church back home, just as you women brought the loaves this morning. Truly, Christianity has a way of drawing us together into one great fellowship. We follow the same God. We love the same Christ. Perhaps the only true line of communication left in the world is the communication of faith, and it will be a tragic day if ever we lose that."

They nodded in understanding. Murmurs of agreement surged along the crowded walls. I could see that my interpreter's words were being relayed from the people in the hallways to the crowds out in the streets. The thought occurred to me that dealing with the Russian people is better than dealing with Russia. We may condemn the leaders, but we can have only a true affection and sympathy for those they lead.

I spoke of my research in other religions. I commented on the warmth and understanding and sincere friendliness of this congregation which had come here for the same reason that people come to church everywhere: to satisfy the quest for God, a quest which cannot be sublimated in anything except God.

There was a great display of emotion when I said I would carry the memory of this service back to America. People touched their hands to their hearts. When I closed with the promise to take their greetings to the churches in my country they responded with excited and enthusiastic waving of hands and murmurs of "God bless you" and "Peace."

Then Pastor Karev announced that the congregation and choir would sing a hymn. He said he hoped it would span the continents and linger with me as I continued my travels. I have heard "God Be with You Till We Meet Again" sung in many places and in many languages, but never with more sincerity and spirit than here in the Moscow Baptist Church. Tears filled the eyes of many worshipers. I looked over to where Lorena was standing and saw her with head bowed and eyes closed. For the moment, cameras were forgotten.

Just then I had the impression that religion in Russia is considerably more vital, more militant, and more real than I had ever believed it could be. The true force of the Russian soul, questing and unconquered, emerged from this congregation, and I felt the spirit of the millions who have persistently refused to let Communism destroy their will to believe. For one brief moment, all that I had seen and heard among the religious people of the Soviet Union blended into a hymn of praise that had something to sing about: faith in religion's tomorrow. The door of hope had been opened and the glory of worship here expressed was a challenge to us who have never had that door forcibly closed.

But, later, after the singing was stilled and after the last earnest worshiper had pressed my hand or said his emotional *"Slava Bogu,"* I walked again near the Kremlin walls. Again I saw the huge crowds passing through the tomb of Stalin and Lenin. Once more, as I realized that religion is still officially deplored and openly denounced by those who rule and control the people, I felt that God

213

is having no easy time of it, no matter what the signs may say.

I remembered what a Russian Roman Catholic said to me, "The Master desperately needs help. That is nothing new. That has been His lot in every nation and in every age. But if you were ever disappointed with the evidence of spirituality in Russia, it is because you did not look deeply enough. Faith here is a subterranean stream and it rises nearer the surface day by day."

How true his observation was, and how strong and clear that stream will again flow in Russian life, only time will tell. But while the Soviet's atheistic experiment continues, and while the churches struggle on, all Russia is watching America for evidences of the impact of our spirituality upon our individual and national life.

That, too, is part of the challenge to you and to me as we reappraise our own faith in the light of the Soviets and God.